MW00906933

Embellishments
for Paper Crafts

was easy to love—an ebon-haired angel
with gigantic brown eyes
irrepressible buoyancy,
and a dimple that made Zeke's heart melt
every time she smiled.

Rosie

Embellishments
for Paper Crafts

Ideas, Tips & Techniques

Pam Klassen and Leslie Conron Carola

HUGH LAUTER LEVIN ASSOCIATES, INC.

© 2006 Hugh Lauter Levin Associates, Inc.
htp://www.HLLA.com
ISBN-10: 0-88363-708-1
ISBN-13: 978-0-88363-708-1

CONCEPT AND DEVELOPMENT: LESLIE CONRON CAROLA, ARENA BOOKS ASSOCIATES, LLC
DESIGN: ELIZABETH JOHNSBOEN, JOHNSBOEN DESIGN

Projects are credited to designers on page.

Printed in Hong Kong.

Distributed by Publishers Group West.

ACKNOWLEDGMENTS
Thank you to the participants—individual designers, artists, crafters, and manufacturers—for their generous contributions to this project. Becky Baack; Jenna Beegle; Patti Behan; Heather Boling; Dave Brethauer; Sherry Cartwright; Shelly Fuhr; Karen Gerbrandt; Rachael Giallongo; Michelle Graden; Jackie Hull; Adrienne Kennedy from My Sentiments Exactly!; MaryAnn Klassen; Pam Klassen; Marla Kress; Kortney Langley; Nathalie Métivier, Marie-France Perron, and Marie Eve Trudeau from Magenta Rubber Stamps; Patricia Milazzo; Alexis Seabrook; Irene Seifer, Kim Smith, and Stacey Turachek from The Great American Stamp Store; Christine Timmons; Michelle Tardie; Trish Turay; Jan Williams.

Jacket image credits: Top left: Jan Williams; bottom left: Shelley Fuhr; top middle: Jackie Hull; bottom middle: Jamie Kilmartin; top right: Christine Timmons; middle right: Jenna Beegle; bottom right: Becky Baack.
Back jacket: Jan Williams.

Contents

Introduction

Wait until you see what paper crafters are using to embellish their projects. You are in for a treat. Ribbons, wires, string, seashells, plastic pieces, bottle caps, brads, eyelets, charms, fabric, rubber stamping, quilling. What would you think to use if you wanted to embellish a scrapbook page or a greeting card or gift wrap? Ribbons? Yes. Brads or eyelets? Absolutely. Dried flowers, a seashell? Yes. Bird feathers? Well, that *is* unusual, but a project we have using them is delightful (below right, by Christine Timmons). But so are coin holders and tin can lids, metal snaps, melted beeswax, and embroidery. It's hard not to be imaginative when you see such possibilities!

Embellishments add color, weight, and texture to your paper craft projects. The idea is to add a little extra style—some spice— to your scrapbook pages, cards, or other projects. We all want to tell a good story, and one of the ways we do so is with our craft projects. Sometimes that means adding an extra detail here or there. Or sometimes it means throwing caution to the wind and creating something outrageous. And that's a good thing! Take some time to sit and dream; imagine what would be the most fun for you.

We have organized *Embellishments for Paper Crafts* around the type of materials used to embellish projects: materials from the natural world (leaves, flowers, seashells, pebbles, sea glass); paper (cardstock, vellum, corrugated cardboard, chipboard); fabric (ribbon, fiber, small pieces of fabric, yarn, thread, lace, rickrack); glass and plastic (buttons, beads, glitter, geometric shapes); and metal (grommets, brads, eyelets, tags, charms, buttons, metal stickers, and wire). Within these sections we include projects ranging from scrapbook pages and albums (large and small) to cards, invitations, gift tags, place cards, gift wrap, boxes, bags, and so on. You will see that many of the projects included in *Embellishments for Paper Crafts* could be in almost any other chapter than the one in which we have placed them. Projects

in each chapter range from simple to complex. We may have wanted to focus on one component, but several techniques or special materials might have been used in the project creation and the project could therefore be included in another chapter. Our aim is to flood your vision and imagination with embellishment possibilities to inspire creative thinking. (See the project above right

from Magenta: a double picture frame with many layers of color rubbed into a surface decorated with beads and metal stickers.)

Haven't seen a friend from long ago? A surprise scrapbook page using a vintage photo and lace, like the one at left created by Pam Klassen, is a grand ice breaker. What would make you smile? If you create a project that makes you smile, chances are quite good that the recipient will feel the same way. The key to successful embellishing is simple: Enjoy yourself, and choose the decorative components from your heart. Paper crafting is a creative way to communicate, and it is fun. Whether you are creating a scrapbook page, a gift card or invitation, gift wrap, or a folded album, even a label for a jar or tin, or Christmas tree ornaments—whatever you are creating—remember the smaller, quieter moments in your life and celebrate those. Crafting is about celebrating life.

Although you shouldn't feel pressured to create perfection, you should strive for good design. The term "design" simply means the arrangement of elements on a page—or how you choose and organize your materials—and you should strive for harmonious composition. Harmonious elements in design are like harmony in music or the natural world: they just feel right. The hard-and-fast rules are few, but good design generally relies on pleasing line, rhythm, contrast, and composition, along with harmonious colors. (See the layered, dry embossed, cut, and embroiderery stitched card by Irene Seifer, above.)

A simple recipe for success in creating any paper craft project is to choose a color scheme, create a balanced composition with a focal point and perspective, and add embellishments. The embellishments can be as simple as a mat or two of co-ordinating colors or as complex as multiple layers of folded papers, ribbons, eyelets, buttons, or special stitching. Or how about altering a coin holder to create an album of photographs housed in an Altoid tin? (See the charming "Liam" project by Marla Kress, opposite.)

Who of us has not embellished a story to make it more interesting? Paper crafters embellish their pages or cards with decorative accents to "lift them up," to add style and visual interest. Selecting items to add to your cards, gift wrap, or album pages is a wonderfully creative prospect. Try something unexpected, like embroidery on paper (see the lovely ribbon rose card by Irene Seifer at right).

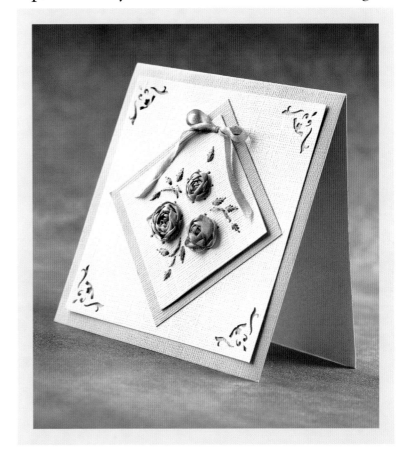

You can create dazzling special effects just by adding simple decorative accents to even the simplest design. We love to combine colors and textures that catch and reflect light from a variety of surfaces. Some send shimmering colors in all directions, some capture and hold the color, some add shine, some add fibrous texture.

Decorative embellishments from sometimes-surprising sources can turn a simple project into a stunning work of art. A recent explosion of decorative materials for paper crafters has produced an exciting assortment of fibers, metallic pieces, special paper products, buttons, and bows that can turn your one-dimensional art into three-dimensional creative delights. Look around you. If something appeals to you, try it. It may not be anything you would find in a craft store, but it may suit your creative expression perfectly. And that is what crafting is all about. The world is your oyster.

Don't forget to have fun!

The Natural World

***

Reach for the stars! Reach for the moon. And reach for sand, stones, seashells, sea grass, twigs, leaves, flowers, and natural fibers. Take a walk on a beach, or in a city park, or in the country to gather natural materials for your paper craft projects. Or look for small baskets, bone buttons, or natural wood frames as you browse in special shops or in your grandmother's attic. There is such an abundance of natural objects to contribute texture and color and weight that the possibility for creating unique, one-of-a-kind, paper craft projects is limitless.

Would you think to enhance your projects with melted beeswax? Or to decorate a small quail egg with colorful paper? You might have fun decorating a paper project with natural materials like a shell or dried flowers or bird feathers, or decorating a natural object, such as a quail egg, with quilled paper flowers. Or how about a down-to-earth bean-covered journal? Or consider the lovely soft effect of a wax coating on a stretched-canvas memory project. We have them all in these pages. And you can adapt the ideas and techniques to your own.

See beyond the individual item to its grandest possibilities. And stretch your imagination. You'll have fun!

NATURE'S HARMONIES

PAINTED AND COLLAGE-FRAMED CARDS | *Pam Klassen*

A rich palette of burnt orange, goldenrod, brown, and fern green provides the base for these earthy cards. Stunning collaged slide mounts frame the centered found objects—leaves, twigs, and a stalk—drawing our eyes to the central focal point. The texture and tone of the natural objects is echoed and supported in the texture and color of the paint and the adorned frames. Look closely at the frames to see an ingenious variety of techniques from stamping to layering torn papers, natural fabric, journaling panels, beads, and even a tiny metal frame.

Creating the Project

1. Apply a thick coating of water-based paint to the front of each card.

2. Wrap the slide mounts in white and printed paper. Add additional material to the frames in a complementary palette, and apply a thin coating of paint as desired. Attach ribbons and twine.

3. Mount one found natural object—leaf, stalk, or a row of twigs—on white cardstock, and trim to fit inside the frame. Attach to the backside of the frame.

4. Place the decorated, framed image just above center on the card front.

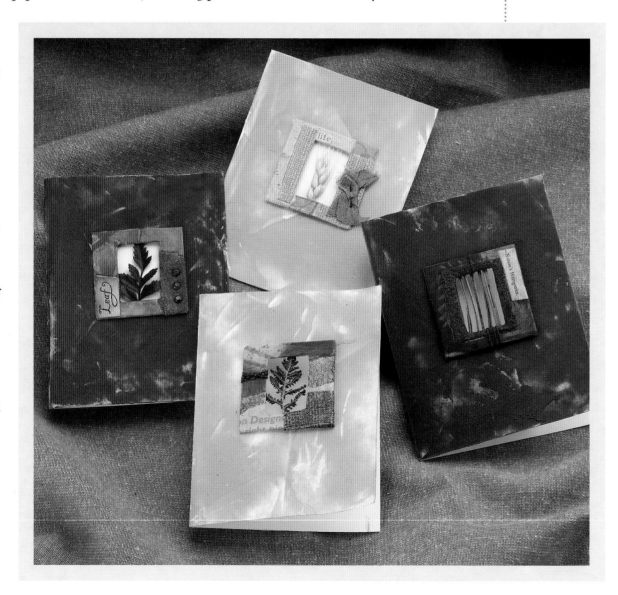

NATURE

DECORATED KEEPSAKE BOX | *Kortney Langley*

A perfect gift for the young botanist in the family. Collaged sheets of botanical images from a book or magazine are placed across the surface of the background paper, but the focal point is the layered panel atop the box. The dimensional letters spelling out "Nature" on this panel are created out of nature's own bounty, in the form of twigs, leaves, a feather, pebbles, and a dried flower.

Creating the Project

1. Tear fairly large pieces of printed paper and adhere to the surface of the box and lid using a decoupage technique.

2. Tear a piece of corrugated cardboard, and mat on black cardstock. Attach the panel to the box lid.

3. Ink the edges of a cream cardstock panel, pulling some of the color across the cardstock, and center it on top of the matted panel.

4. Gather nature's items that mimic the shape of the letters—see above. Glue items to the mat, spelling "Nature." Add sticker letters and tie leather cord around lid.

TWO CARDS/TAG

GARDEN GATE / GARDEN CENTER CARD | *Jackie Hull*

A wonderful old key —the key to the garden gate—captures our eye and leads it directly down to the peacock feather flared beneath it. Off-white, moss green, slate blue, and black with a rich claret-ribbon highlight provide the lush palette for an engaging card/tag on the left. The intriguing quote sets the wishful tone.

Creating the Project

1. Cut two pieces of manila folder into tag shapes, one large and one small (or use two commercial manila tags).

2. Stamp a leaf pattern in moss green and slate blue near the edges of both tags, as shown.

3. Print the quote on your printer, tear the edges, and angle it across the smaller tag.

4. Lightly coat the surface of both cards with gold ink (using a direct-to-paper technique).

5. Glue the peacock feather onto the large card. Layer the smaller card on top, aligning the punched holes. Slip a ribbon through the two holes, and through the ring of the key.

The green garden center card on the right is edged in silver, with leaves stamped in silver on the green card and on the lavender mat. The four-color printed card on top is finished with an unevenly cut piece of clear acetate layered over it and tied with gold ribbon.

FLIP-FLOPS

MEMORY BOX | *Trish Turay*

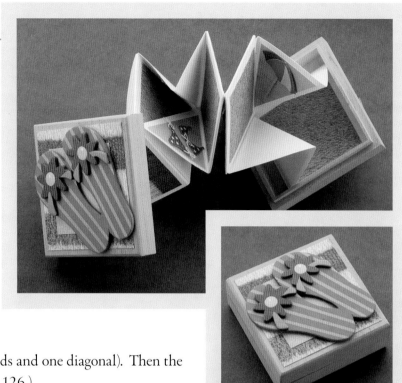

$\mathscr{A}$ wooden box made to hold summer's memories. The wooden flip-flops that adorn the top of this box recall days of summer fun. The pages inside fold out to hold the memorabilia. What a great idea for a gift to present to a friend headed off on vacation. The album is ready for the photos and journaling.

Creating the Project

1. Paint the box and let it dry completely.

2. Adhere two squares of patterned paper to the top of the box. Glue wooden flip-flops onto the paper at an angle.

3. The inside pages are created with a simple fold (two book folds and one diagonal). Then the folded squares are attached together. (See the template on page 126.)

HAPPY SUMMER

CARD | *Kim Smith*

$\mathscr{T}$ he beach is created with paper and Make It Stone Sandy Beach spray paint. The card is simple and cheerful. Two delicate seashells are sitting on the sand, just waiting for collection!

Creating the Project

1. Spray paint a sheet of cardstock with Make It Stone Sandy Beach. Tear the edge and layer onto the baseline of a blue cardstock panel $\frac{1}{2}$ inch smaller all around than a white card. (We have used a 5 x 7-inch card and a 4 $\frac{1}{2}$ x 6 $\frac{1}{2}$-inch blue panel.)

2. Add the beach chair and umbrella. Place the seashells on the sand.

FLOWER POWER

NOTEBOOK | *Trish Turay*

A long column of brightly colored ribbons tied at quirky angles lends a carefree, festive note to this charming notebook cover. Nature does offer flowers in a rainbow of bright colors, but in this case brightly colored wooden flowers are used to quickly decorate a notebook.

Creating the Project

1. Layer cardstock squares in the center of the cover.

2. Glue wooden flowers to the center.

3. Cut several lengths of bright ribbons and tie to the binding at jaunty angles.

BLOOMING

BAG | *Patricia Milazzo*

A ny gift will be made extra special with a thoughtful personalized gift bag complete with an inspirational sentiment attached. Accent the wooden tags with colored pencil and highlight with liquid embossing before tying them onto the bag. The soft palette is effective.

Creating the Project

1. Cut blue patterned paper to fit within the front panel of a small natural-color shopping bag, and ink the edges. Glue the panel to the front of the bag.

2. Cut a piece of violet cardstock and ink the edges with a coordinating color ink. Print the quote on the cardstock, and attach it to the bag with brads.

3. Color two wooden tags with watercolor pencils. Apply liquid embossing over the floral image to highlight it.

4. Attach tags together with a brad and pin onto the ribbons tied to the bag handles.

SEARCHING 4 BURIED TREASURE

ALBUM | *Patricia Milazzo*

A tan linen album cover is embellished with striped paper, wood tags brandishing seashore decorations, paper panels, and several ribbons. The carefree, natural palette supports the spirit of the project. The simple black-and-white photo in the deeply recessed frame shouts of casual summer days. The album comes with the recessed frame on the cover. The linen edges have been inked to the color of wet sand. Sunny summer-colored striped paper with inked edges covers the front of the album. Coordinating papers are used for a mat at the top right, for the numeral 4, and for a horizontal panel across the base.

"GONE FISHING"

SCRAPBOOK PAGE | *Sherry Cartwright*

A rugged masculine layout with an outdoor theme is achieved with a border of torn cardboard and nature's own materials. This design idea would also work well for a day at the zoo or a trip to the park.

Creating the Project

1. Tear off one side of patterned paper, ink the edges of the remaining piece, and attach to a light brown cardstock sheet. Offset a smaller piece of lighter brown cardstock on top of the patterned paper.

2. Mount the two fishing photos to the page on top of the layered papers, and adhere stickers. Tear a strip of corrugated cardboard, cover it with a light coat of white acrylic paint, and ink all of the edges.

3. Attach eyelets through each end of the cardboard and tie with hemp. Add a stamped canvas tag. Layer nature stickers, magic mesh, and feathers and secure to the border with decorative tack.

ENJOY THE MOMENT

CARD | *Patricia Milazzo*

A small file folder becomes the perfect card to congratulate a workplace promotion. Inks, distressed paper, a trio of paper flowers, and a wooden frame tied to the folder with an old-fashioned ribbon give an earthy, slightly nostalgic look to this creative card.

Creating the Project

1. Trim an off-white card into a file-folder shape with a tab.

2. Ink all edges of the card with warm brown ink. Cut blocks of patterned paper, ink the edges, and adhere to the card front, back, and inside.

3. Back a chipboard letter and mount it on a printed paper block. Stamp the selected words on the panel. Tint the wood frame with ink and mount "Congrats" on paper behind the frame.

4. Attach the frame to the card with ribbon, brads, and staples. Attach brads to the centers of three flowers and glue to the card.

YOU @ 2

TAG | *Marla Kress*

A little wooden framed photo mounted on this tag is etched with the words that depict a two-year-old's feisty, nay-saying attitude. A great reminder for the two-year-old that he is loved everyday, even when he and the rest of the world are not in synch.

Creating the Project

1. Cut a tag from light brown cardstock and round the corners.

2. Print text on the patterned paper, and add the sticker number. Trim patterned paper to the tag size and adhere to the front of the tag.

3. Stain the wooden frame with moss-colored walnut ink, let dry, and layer over the photo. Mount to the tag.

4. Fold a torn muslin strip over the top of the tag and hammer the grommet into the muslin. Tie on the ribbon.

CHRISTMAS

CARD | *Rachael Giallongo*

A flourish of Santa Claus–themed thoughts crowd the dominant frame on this old-fashioned Christmas card. The ball ornament, coated with gold leaf, glows at the center of an open frame mounted on an ageless green and white striped background.

Creating the Project

1. Cut soft green and white patterned paper to fit, and attach to the front of the card. Use a gold-leafing pen to edge the card. Paint a red acrylic line inside the gold edge of the card.

2. Using a small amount of paint on a foam brush, gently wipe red paint over the surface of the wood frame. A gentle touch will prevent the paint from going into the recessed areas of the frame.

3. Color the charm with a gold-leafing pen, tie with ribbon, and adhere inside the frame on the card.

LOVE

CARD | *Rachael Giallongo*

An asymmetric composition of warm tones is reminiscent of a well-composed puzzle. The main canvas is divided into thirds tied together with a bottom border: one vertical red-and-white striped section, and two horizontal patterned sections create the balance. A brick-red rubber frame connects the panels.

Creating the Project

1. Cover a card oriented horizontally with three panels of paper, and add a fourth as a border across the full width of the card at the bottom edge.

2. Attach the brick-red rubber frame with brads to the upper right section.

3. Stamp the word "Love" on a patterned paper panel, and center in the frame.

BEACH MEMORIES

PHOTO FRAME | *Heather Boling*

*R*ecall the wondrous moments of the youngsters—brother and sister hand-in-hand on a water-edge stroll at the beach—each time you look at this beautifully embellished photo frame. Shells, seaweed, and even sand collected from the beach are used to finish this memory-filled project.

Creating the Project

1. Spread glue over the entire surface of the frame and cover generously with sand.

2. Let dry completely and rub off excess sand.

3. Attach shells, sand dollars, and other collected items to the corners of the frame with glue.

SOMETHING BEAUTIFUL

SCRAPBOOK PAGES | *Pam Klassen*

*T*he stamped leaf images bring a glowing quality to a beautiful background for family photos. We used real leaves painted with fall colors to stamp these fine natural world images.

Creating the Project

1. Follow the steps below to paint and stamp the leaf images on the background pages, repeating with different leaf shapes.

2. Tear fabric mats and adhere to the pages.

3. Mount photos on the mats.

4. Attach eyelets and a photo turn, and tie with ribbon.

5. Press and dry leaves. Cover the dry leaves with paint, and glue to the layout. Stamp quote with paint on cardstock; cut out, and adhere to both pages.

Steps for the stamped leaf:

1. Paint the surface of the leaf with an even coat of paint.

2. Lay the leaf paint-side down on the cardstock background sheet and roll over the leaf with a brayer.

GIFT WRAP

STAMPED PAPER WITH BIRD FEATHERS | *Christine Timmons*

*W*ould you ever think to enhance wrapping paper or gift cards with bird feathers? This artist had fun focusing on texture and tone. The palette is outrageous and glorious: brilliant chartreuse, brown, and turquoise. Feathers float across the surface of the gift paper and card, and hang freely from the ends of the ribbon-wrapped box, creating an abundance of delicate texture. (See page 10.)

Creating the Project

1. Using brown ink, stamp several bird nests on the green paper.

2. Add a few eggs in the nests and on the surface of the paper, along with a variety of feather shapes floating around the nests and across the paper in a random pattern.

3. Dab turquoise paint on the brown-stamped eggs. Attach several short lengths of turquoise string.

4. Finish with micro beads.

MOMENTS

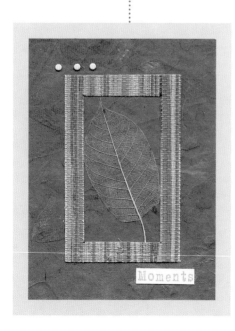

CARD | *Karen Gerbrandt*

*T*his understated card made of natural elements creates a soothing feeling as soon as it is picked up. Mulberry paper and a framed skeleton leaf work together to create a soft textured accent.

Creating the Project

1. Cover the front of the card with mulberry paper, letting the uncut edge of the paper hang off the edge of the card.

2. Cut a frame from straw paper and mount in the middle of the card. Glue a leaf inside the frame.

3. Attach brads above the frame and stamped text below the frame.

4. Finish by adding a thin column of the straw paper down the outside edge of the inside page of the card.

ALBUM COVER

BEAN-COVERED SKETCH BOOK | *Jenna Beegle*

*T*his artist smiles when someone says she is "full of beans!" What a wonderful, down-to-earth cover for an artist's journal. This is also a project that could be adapted to create with children. The technique is very organized, but not difficult, the pattern easy to follow, and the effect wondrous.

Creating the Project

1. Cut two pieces of 9 x 12-inch chipboard for the covers, and cover with brown craft paper.

2. To bind the book line up the interior papers and covers and clamp together. With a small bit, drill three holes through all layers.

3. Draw your design on the cover using a ruler and pencil to create guidelines.

4. Apply a rub-on letter to the center. Glue a watch crystal over the letter.

5. Separate the beans before starting this step. When applying beans to your design, work in small sections. Apply an even coat of glue and quickly arrange the beans one at a time. Allow twenty-four hours for the cover to dry after adhering all the beans. Apply a coat of acrylic sealer following manufacturer's directions for drying time and humidity.

6. Finish binding by tying a ribbon through the drilled holes.

 For an even, uniform effect, make sure the beans are of similar size and condition.

AUGUST TREASURES

SPRAY-AND-STAMP TIN | *Pam Klassen*

*S*crapbooking has leapt out of its covers. Here is a fabulous way to celebrate a summer reunion with a cherished friend, utilizing treasures from nature all the way around—from sea grass and dried flowers to a bone button, starfish, sand dollar, and a tiny wood frame.

Creating the Project

1. Sand well, and then spray the top and bottom of a CD tin and frame with step 1 crackle paint. Let dry.

2. Following manufacturer's directions, spray the top and bottom of the tin three or four times with step 2 crackle paint. Let dry.

3. Stamp calligraphic "August" on the tin top with paint and the remaining words with ink. See the step photo at left.

4. Tie dried flowers to the fabric and adhere to the page. Glue on the frame and remaining items.

JOURNEY

MOUNTED CANVAS | *Kim Smith*

*T*orn background papers, a silhouetted photograph, a brass key, and a transit token are presented on a canvas mounted on a wood frame. The frame is edged with buttons sewn in a tight row. The image is strong, but the wondrous element to this project is the layers of wax which makes us feel that we are looking at something preserved from long ago.

Creating the Project

1. Brush warm beeswax on a stretched canvas with a wide brush.

2. Add torn paper of varying earthy tones, and smooth with a hot iron. Attach Scrabble™ letters spelling out the word "JOURNEY." Add more wax, and iron again.

3. Silhouette and attach the photograph, the brass key, and the token. Color directly on the warm iron with crayons, and then iron the wax surface again.

4. Stitch buttons around all four sides of the frame.

5. Cover the whole front surface with melted wax. Let it dry.

 The crayon wipes off a warm (not hot) iron easily.

Paper

*P*aper is irresistible—rough or smooth, glossy coated or uncoated, translucent or corrugated, thick or thin, foldable or unbendable, it stimulates our senses. For the paper craft artist, it is an infinitely versatile canvas, one that is easy to handle and to store. Paper adds drama and interest to your paper craft creations, or it can also *be* the paper craft.

You can fold, roll, tear, cut, punch, pierce, emboss, weave, stitch, embroider, and generally embellish paper to create an unlimited number of unique effects. Need a dab of bright color quickly? That's easy with colored paper or paper painted, inked, or chalked to meet your palette requirements. There are papers in patterns, colors, textures, and weights for all your paper craft projects, from card-making to scrapbooking, giftwrapping to decorative additions to your home.

We have included projects full of layered texture and color: from magical coiled and crimped objects; decorative punched flowers, pinwheels, and geometric shapes; folded; stamped; layered; torn and stitched paper as well as a delightful product—Paper Perfect™—that produces an extraordinary dimensional surface ready to be shaped and colored.

PASTEL FLOWERS

TEXTURED PICTURE FRAME | *Patti Behan*

*P*aper Perfect ™ is a paint that creates the look of handmade paper when applied to a variety of surfaces with a brush or palette knife. You can apply it to a surface such as a plastic page protector and let it dry overnight. When dry it can be peeled off the plastic sheet just like paper, and cut into a desired shape. This charming white frame is covered with white Paper Perfect™ and then embellished with three layered pastel-colored flowers punched from Paper Perfect™ sheets. Tiny, curled silver wire adorns the centers of the three flowers and serves as jaunty, curved stems.

NEW HOME

TAG SCRAPBOOK | *Trish Turay*

A small personal album made with tags offers images and thoughts about a new home. It brings to mind the work that goes into making it, and the love that fills it.

Creating the Project

1. Ink the ends of tags, tear decorative paper and adhere to the center of the tags.

2. Mount text inside the slide mount; mat a favorite quote and glue to the page.

3. Add thumbnail photos and a ribbon-tied metal heart.

SO LONG, TEXAS

PHOTO WEAVING CARD | *Becky Baack*

A combination of horizontal and vertical strips adds texture and interest to a layered card. Photographs have been scanned into a computer and printed in color. The photograph of the children has been printed twice and layered and woven horizontally, producing a kind of louvered effect.

Creating the Project

1. With a computer, layer a scenery and portrait photo using photo manipulation software. Print two copies.

2. Cut four pieces vertically in varying widths on the long end of the scenery photo. Be sure to keep the photo pieces in order.

3. Make five vertical cuts within one of the portrait pictures, ending at the top and bottom.

4. Cut out four horizontal pieces from the second portrait section to weave through the vertical cuts.

5. Incorporate cut strips of green paper and weave horizontally through the spaced scenery cuts. Extend a section of green paper for handwritten journaling.

6. Adhere the completed woven picture to the card.

TIP *Begin to weave from the center, keeping the pieces tight as you work outwardly. Work by turning from front to back, adhering as you go.*

HAPPY BIRTHDAY

CARD WITH DIMENSIONAL PINWHEEL | *Kim Smith*

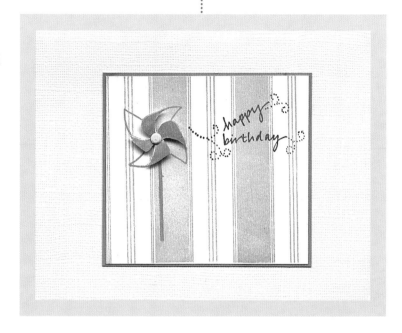

*T*his simple card will remind someone that birthday wishes are blowing their way! The added dimension of the pinwheel lifted from the card surface creates a sense of motion.

Creating the Project

1. Mat blue-and-white striped paper on blue cardstock and adhere to a yellow card. Stamp the pinwheel and sentiment on the front.

2. Stamp the pinwheel a second time and silhouette. Adhere over the center of the stamped pinwheel, "popping" by placing foam mounting tape underneath it.

3. Attach a brad through the center.

THANK YOU

CARD | *Dave Brethauer*

A soft blue palette with minimal accents of green stems is quietly serene. The die-cut paper flowers add gentle texture. You don't always need a big splash to make a big statement!

Creating the Project

1. Stamp a pale blue panel background on a 1 $\frac{1}{8}$ x 4 $\frac{1}{8}$-inch panel of white cardstock.

2. Stamp a green stem and add four flowers punched out of blue cardstock.

3. Punch a small rectangle out of heavy blue cardstock. Stamp the message, and pierce the border holes.

4. Intensify the blue panel with darker blue chalk rubbed on. Keep the edges of the chalked area soft.

HOLLY LEAVES

QUILLED NOTEPAD COVER | *Jan Williams*

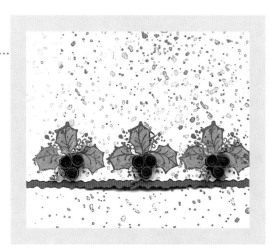

*Q*uilled holly leaves create a festive matchbook-style cover for a Post-It™ notepad, a thoughtful, useful handmade Christmas gift for a favorite teacher or pal.

Creating the Project

1. For a 3 x 3-inch Post-It™ pad, cut a 3 ¼ x 6 ½-inch cover out of sturdy cardstock. Spray or splatter (with an old, ready-to-toss-out toothbrush) red ink over the surface of the cardstock cover. Create fold lines on the cover at the top and bottom edges of the pad. Fold on the fold lines.

2. Cut a 1-inch piece of red paper to the same width as the cover, and cut the edge with deckle scissors. Cut the top edge of the cover with the same deckle scissors. Layer the red paper on the back side of the front cover, leaving a ⅛-inch border. Stamp three sets of holly leaves across the surface just above the red border. Color the holly leaves with a green marker.

3. Roll tight red coils for the holly berries and glue in place. Add small green curls as vines.

4. Attach a velcro circle inside the top cover and below on the inside cover. Stick the notepad inside the covers.

THE NATURE

PRINTED CHIPBOARD | *Rachael Giallongo*

A muted, old-world palette speaks of the natural order. The sophisticated palette of harmonious colors ties together the many elements in the project— paper, plastic, ribbon, chipboard. The uneven type stamped at the bottom of the panel echoes the wind-blown look of the angled letter panel above.

Creating the Project

1. Separate the alphabet stencil. Paint the N with green acrylic paint, ink the edges with black to create contrast, and set aside.

2. Paint the stencil negative with purple paint. Add ribbon at the side of the negative panel and attach the plastic word label.

3. Paint the edges of the cardstock block and the stamped quote, highlighting the word "Nature" by stamping it on a piece of painted cardstock.

4. Add stickers to the border of the card and attach the chipboard letter.

5. Finish by painting the card edge and attaching the cardstock block.

CATS

SCRAPBOOK PAGE WITH DIMENSIONAL PAINT | *Pam Klassen*

*W*hat could be more intriguing than a cat? When creating a page of your favorite feline, use dimensional paint to provide a quick medium that produces an eye-catching textured embellishment. This well-composed page is easy, colorful, and imaginative.

Creating the Project

1. Brayer two shades of yellow acrylic paint over the page background. Mount photos to the page.

2. Follow the steps below to create the dark-blue-and-yellow dimensional paint embellishments. Cut into four square and two circle shapes and glue to the page, as shown. Glue fabric flowers to the embellished squares and accent with buttons.

Steps:

1. Using a palette knife spread a thin, even coat of dark-blue dimensional paint over the surface of yellow paper.

2. Press down firmly with the texture comb and drag through the surface of the paint, to create texture.

TIP *Try dragging several household items in the dimensional paint to create different textured embellishments.*

TIED TOGETHER

FRAMED CARD DUO| *Jackie Hull*

Two elegantly simple expressions of love. Left: A romantic anniversary card in a soft violet and yellow palette with stamped flowers, a delicate ribbon, and a secret letter. (A small yellow card is folded and tucked inside a pocket folded from muted floral paper and placed at the bottom of the card.) Right: A wonderful photograph of three boys looking straight at us from inside a framed window—a moment to remember and cherish. The natural putty-colored paint over the orange echoes the colors in the photo. The violet photo corners add a bright touch. The rainbow ribbon and feather tied on to the top of the card are a cheerful complement to the whole. Both of these charming cards are about texture and tone.

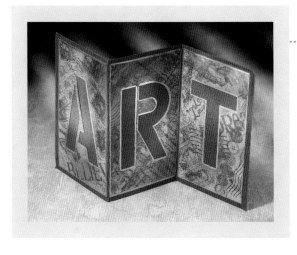

ART

FOLDED STENCIL CARD | *Kim Smith*

This "ART" card, made with Classic Lettering Stencils™, is fast and easy to make with great results. Accordion-fold dark cardstock into three pages, each page being slightly larger than the stencil letter. Randomly stamp the surface of each of the stencils with a variety of memorabilia images. Stipple to add color, using a brush and inkpads. Outline each letter and the outside edge of the stencil sheet with a gold-leafing pen. Mount the stencils to the folded cardstock.

SOCCER BUDS

TAG | *Becky Baack*

T‍he creative use of the photos on this high-energy tag makes them an inspirational embellishment. The palette and the repetitive use of the tag shape in the two satellite photos contribute to the overall success of the composition. This technique would work with photos of any theme.

Creating the Project

1. Cut the large tag from cardstock. Tear paper and the top of the main photo. Layer the paper strips and photo on the tag, and machine-stitch all layers to the tag.

2. Create text and decorative borders with pens.

3. Cut black-and-white photos into tags freehand, or by using a pattern, machine-stitching along the bottom. Tie small photo tags to the large tag with fibers. The small photos can be tucked behind the layered papers on the large tag, or left loose.

SNOWFLAKE

UNFOLDING HOLIDAY CARD | *Kim Smith*

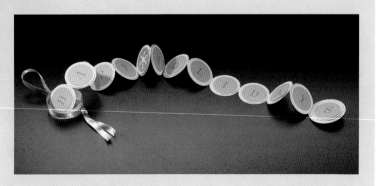

W‍hat a great idea for a card—an unfolding row of tiny punched layered circles tumbling out of a small plastic container wrapped with elegant ribbon. Each circle bears a letter to spell out "Happy Holidays," and one for a snowflake. The technique is simple, and could be adapted for many effects. Four panels of lime-green paper are accordion-folded into a stack of five segments each. A small circle is punched through each stack. The stacks are connected by layering the last circle from one to the first circle of the next. Individual small blue circles are punched out with a smaller punch and glued on top of each of the lime-green circles.

DOORCAT

CAT SILHOUETTE FOR DOOR FRAME | *Nathalie Métivier*

$\mathcal{T}$his delightful heavy-cardboard embellished doorcat silhouette from Magenta is handsome and imaginative. Front and back are decorated so that he can move from one side of the door (or shelf or window frame) to the other. He brings feline elegance and charm to any room décor!

Creating the Project *For the tan side:*

1. Cover one edge of the cat with stickers, positioning the flowers and leaves to create a nicely balanced effect. Overlap some patterns, and leave space between others. We created a sort of flower collar with a large flower sticker. Let some stickers run off the edge of the cat and trim off the extra with scissors or a craft knife. Color the rest of the cat with amber and brown-tone Cat's Eyes™. The amber color can overlap and color between the stickers. The darker tones are mostly for the edges of the cat.

2. Add some self-adhesive copper dot and circle and mini flower Peel Off's to enhance the project. Finish with stickers and glossy accents.

The darkest colors are applied mostly to the edges to give some dimension to the cat.

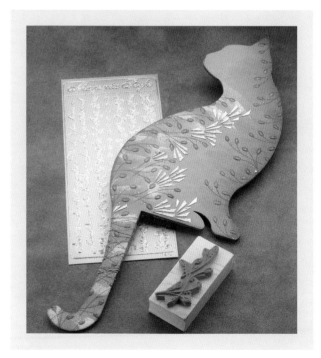

For the turquoise side:

1. Using a direct-to-paper technique, color the cat starting with the lightest colors and working to the darkest one. In order, use: Seaglass, Mint, Aqua, and Teal Cat's Eyes™. Then the three MicaMagic™ colors: Lime Gloss, Bright Blue, and Black. Stroke the MicaMagic™ colors out to the edges, trying to resemble a cat's fur. Stamp the branch image along the edges with deep-green chalk pad, and enhance with colored pencil and glossy accents. Set aside to dry.

2. Self-adhesive aluminum embellishments can be used as is, or colored. Here, they are roughly colored with a gold-leafing pen. Let dry. Cut with scissors into tiny sticky pieces that are easy to display to enhance the pattern.

3. Wrap very thin double-sided tape around the cat's tail. Wrap a few gold maruyama threads around the cat's tail over the tape. The gold threads will adhere instantly to the tape.

MESSAGE CENTER

EMBELLISHED BLACKBOARD | *Karen Gerbrandt*

This project becomes more than a simple blackboard. It is a real design statement. This message center now holds photos, cards, keys, and more. It can be covered in paper to coordinate with any child's room.

Creating the Project

1. Paint the tray at the bottom of the blackboard and three small clothespins with acrylic paint and let dry. Glue printed paper to cover the frame.

2. Color twill tape with ink, tie, and attach to the frame with tacks. The twill will hold in place any special notes, invitations, or school assignments you need to keep in view.

3. Glue a silk flower to each painted clothespin and add buttons for the centers. Glue decorated clothespins to the frame.

FLIPPER

SCRAPBOOK PAGE | *Jan Williams*

*S*tamped images create movement across a page when they are silhouetted, cut, and then layered slightly off-center.

Creating the Project

1. Brayer ink on a dolphin stamp and stamp the image on paper. Before re-inking, stamp the image a second time onto the background page, creating a "ghost" image. Continue this process until the background page is filled.

2. Crop and mat photos, journaling circle, and title circle and mount onto the background page.

3. Silhouette eight of the original stamped dolphin images. Adhere two dolphins together, offsetting slightly the top image of each pair.

4. Add matted photos and two circles of journaling in a pleasing arrangement.

5. Use foam adhesive to pop the images on the page in a lively arc.

ENJOY LIFE'S MOMENTS / SIBLINGS

LAYERED CARD DUET | *Jackie Hull*

Two nostalgic cards remind us of what's important—enjoy life's moments, both quiet and loud, and cherish a sister's love. Sentimental, yes, and heart warming. The cards are full of layered texture and color, and wrapped with warmth and memories.

Left: The strong centered design of the "Life's Moments" card features a tall corrugated cardboard strip enhanced with color and glitter, wrapped and tied with gift paper and ribbon, and layered onto a gold-edged mat mounted on a burgundy card. Atop the cardboard strip is a pink heart embossed with gold and finished with an amber glass bead. The harmonious, rich colors support the message and enhance the design.

Right: An old-fashioned image of two Victorian-era girls is stamped using opaque pastel colors on a tag inked with a direct-to-paper technique. Old-fashioned, small white buttons, lace, and soft ribbon adorn the ageless card/tag.

ATTRIBUTE PHOTOGRAPHY

SCRAPBOOK PAGE | *Marla Kress*

*A*s a scrapbooker, the purpose of a layout is to showcase the photographs, but in this case, with a little creative manipulation, the photos become the embellishment itself.

Creating the Project

1. Create the right side of the page by machine-stitching striped and paisley papers together with a zigzag stitch. Attach to the top of the page and print photos to fill the space beneath.

2. Print text on vellum and glue to the left side of the page; fill the bottom edge with a paisley print. Wrap ribbon around the page, attaching at back.

3. With a photo-editing computer program, create the letter "A" in a 3¼-inch block font. Layer photos within the "A" shape, print, and cut out.

4. Adhere the "A" on the stitched square with computer journaling. Place the square over the ribbon and attach flowers with small brads.

RIBBIT

SCRAPBOOK PAGE | *Jan Williams*

*T*wo-toned die-cut frogs with quilled paper centers hop over the surface of this charming, summer-day scrapbook page. Torn-edged beige corners assert energy and pull—frogs on one, and the title and a lone frog on the other. A little girl in pink, holding her frog (prince) takes center stage. The palette is classic frog and little girl.

Creating the Project

1. Cut a 6-inch square of cardstock and use a blow pen (or an old toothbrush) to spatter with ink. Tear the spattered cardstock against a deckle-edge ruler to create two triangles. Mat each piece with a darker color and attach them in opposite corners of the page.

2. Cut out frog die cuts, alternating front and back body colors. Accent the faces with pen work.

3. Quill loose coils and fit to the shape of the frog's body. Assemble all frogs and adhere to the corners.

4. Mount photos, print journaling, and attach to the page. Layer die-cut letters to fit in the lower corner.

PURPLE FLOWER

QUILLED MOSAIC TAG | *Jan Williams*

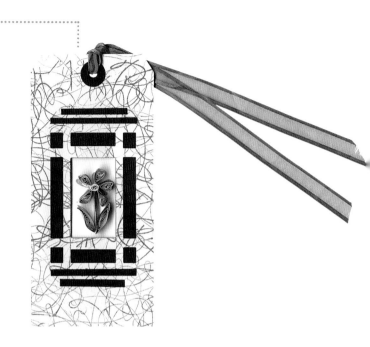

A purple mosaic-like pre-cut tag frames a single flower—a beautiful accent for an elegant scrapbook design or graceful special gift. The pre-cut tag offers a stained-glass effect and supports an elegant quilled flower.

Creating the Project

1. Select a tag with a mosaic-like die-cut frame. Stamp the surface with a scribble stamp (or do your own scribbling!). Back the tag with purple cardstock, and turn it over to the front. Cut the purple cardstock from the center rectangular opening. Glue the tag onto white cardstock cut to the same size.

2. Stamp a flower in the center rectangle in gray ink, and quill teardrop shapes to match the petals. Add marquise shapes for the leaves.

3. Finish with a punched cardstock reinforcement for the hole at the top tied with a ribbon.

YOU ARE INVITED

INVITATION | *Becky Baack*

*T*earing and stitching give a unique touch to this birthday-party invitation. Printed "Happy Birthday" paper is stitched with rows of bright torn paper looking like waves. A small matted photograph of the birthday girl adorns the front, personalizing the cheery invitation with style.

Creating the Project

1. Lay the printed "Happy Birthday" paper over a plain white card front. Tear strips of bright blue cardstock and lay in rows across the front.

2. Machine-stitch along the strips through all thicknesses.

3. Add text to the scanned photo, mat with pink cardstock, and mount on the card front.

MAGENTA EMBELLISHMENTS

FOLDED CARD | *Nathalie Métivier*

A lovely blue card folded over to hold a double-sided stamped and colored annex. Maruyama paper, gold thread, and Magenta's gold embellishments add the finishing touch.

Creating the Project

1. Stamp a column of floral images on two sheets of paper. Stamp one image at the top, and a different image just below that, leaving about a ¼-inch space between the two stamped images. Add the third image, a repeat of the first one leaving about a ¼-inch space between image two and three. Trim the stamped column leaving a border of about ¼ inch to the edge of the panel. Color the stamped images with soft-colored pencils.

2. See the drawing on page 126. Draw a pencil line 2 ¾ inches in from the right side and cut on the line leaving ¼ inch at the top and bottom still attached. Extend the cut line 1 inch to the right. Open the card so that it looks like the photo at middle right. Add the stamped panels back-to-back overlapping about 1 ½ inches of the folded edge of the blue card.

3. Attach a wide strip of maruyama blue paper at the left edge of the card front, and tucked just under the left edge of the folded-back panel.

4. Decorate the folded-back panel with a gold sticker vine, and a gold sticker flower attached to light green paper. Finish with gold filaments bunched and tucked under the edge of the flower sticker.

NEW YEAR'S EVE

FESTIVE DECORATIONS | *Patti Behan*

$\mathcal{F}$estively wrapped items—a gift package and cracker, napkin ring, and place card—are ready for a New Year's Eve celebration. The box bottom is wrapped in silver and the top is covered with a woven paper arrangement of plain and dappled silver paper. The ribbon is organza with silver dots. The same ribbon carries over to both the cracker—ready to be popped at midnight—and the place card. Accents of gold appear on the napkin ring and place card. The palette is celebratory and consistent: predominantly silver, followed by blue, and finally the gold accent. Not a lot, not difficult, but thoughtful and festive.

LOVE

FOUR-SQUARE CARD | *Pam Klassen*

$\mathcal{T}$he soft look of handmade paper embellishes this beautiful card for a sweetheart. Special paint available in a variety of colors is a quick alternative to making paper.

Creating the Project

1. Cut four chipboard letter blocks using a pattern. Follow the steps below to cover the chipboard with handmade paper and stamp.

2. Place blocks spaced evenly on the card front. Use double-sided adhesive to secure the squares onto the card and the paper flowers inside the openings.

Steps

1. Working on a plastic sheet, use a palette knife to spread a thin, even coat of Paper Perfect™ over the chipboard shapes. Cover all edges.

2. While Paper Perfect™ is still wet, use paint and foam stamps, pressing letters into the mixture to create depth.

3. Let the squares dry twelve to twenty-four hours until completely dry. Trim the edges. If the chipboard warps, weight it down with heavy books to straighten.

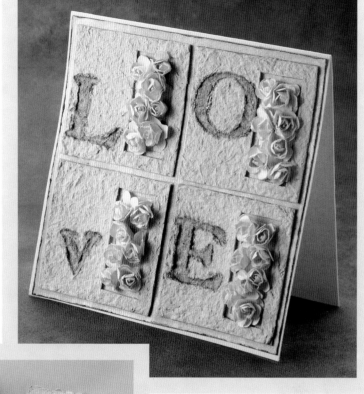

TIP *If you make a mistake while stamping, wipe off mixture, remix, and start over.*

WINTER

SCRAPBOOK PAGE | *Marla Kress*

old wintry elements stretch across this frosty layout, from snow-laden trees and ground to a red-cheeked youngster in his snowsuit, to the possibility of mugs of warming cocoa with marshmallows. Wood tags are used to embellish the text and label the themed photos.

Creating the Project

1. Attach photos to each side of the page. Add a printed journaling block on the left and blue cardstock down the center. Layer strips of patterned paper across the top and bottom, and dotted paper across the seams.

2. Print the title in reverse onto cardstock, cut out, and glue down the center of the page.

3. Dry-brush the etched wooden tags with blue paint, add brads, and adhere to the page. Use white rub-on letters to extend the tag words.

WELCOME, BABY

BABY SCRAPBOOK | *Heather Boling*

ive depth to die-cut shapes by adding decorative quilled centers. These little die-cut animal shapes—a pig, rabbit, chick, and teddy bear—with quilled centers add dimension and a spirit of fun to this charming scrapbook page announcing the birth of a baby. The textured blue-diamond mats beneath the die-cut quilled figures echo the patterned-paper background.

A-TISKET, A-TASKET

BASKET WITH QUILLED PAPER FLOWER | *Jan Williams*

*T*he centerpiece of this mini-basket is the cheerful yellow daisy on the lid, quilled with narrow strips of yellow and green paper. Loose coils and marquise shapes form the petals. A marquise shape is simply a loose coil flattened slightly between your thumb and forefinger to form a point at each end.

Creating the Project

1. Spatter ink to softly color the outside of the basket.

2. Use a paper crimper to crimp paper strips before rolling into desired shapes.

3. Roll loose paper coils on a quilling tool and then allow the coil to relax and expand to the desired size. Glue the end of the strip to the coil. Create marquise shapes for leaves and teardrops for petals. (See page 51.)

4. Attach petals to a 1-inch base coil.

5. Layer 24 inches of soft and bright yellow quilling strips and fringe the length. Roll into a coil and attach the fringe side up.

TIP *Work gently when rolling crimped paper into shapes, so the crimping is not removed.*

STAR ORNAMENT

QUILLED STAR | *Jan Williams*

*T*his stunning Christmas-tree ornament is something you can make for your own Christmas tree and for any lucky friends or extended family members. This will be a gift that lasts for years and years. A purchased wood star ornament is painted gold and covered with tiny quilled coils. The quilled shapes are all tight coils—not difficult to make, but the sheer number of them is awesome!

FAR-AWAY DESTINATION

ALTERED BOOK | *Kim Smith*

*D*isplay a sampling of your favorite paper-craft techniques within the covers of an old, ready-to-be-discarded book refreshed with some of your own cherished mementos. Altered books give new life to old books and interesting creative opportunities to the paper crafter. Look at these altered books for the ideas, and then adapt the techniques to suit your themes and interests.

Creating the Project

1. Color the surface of the facing pages by stippling or a direct-to-paper technique, and collage the double-page spread with interesting paper objects in a consistent beige-and-brown palette.

2. Add color copies of silhouetted old-fashioned instruments—sextant, compass, globe—and a few large tags in a postcard folder.

3. Place a large printed paper triangle on the lower right corner and attach an articulated paper doll cut from coordinating printed paper, and attach to the page with silver brads.

WINDOW PAGE

ALTERED BOOK | *Kim Smith*

*T*he pages of an altered book can hold all sorts of treasured items, from tickets to advertisements torn from magazines or newspapers to a musical score. The sophisticated brown page with a cut-circle window is filled with an old portrait drawing printed on acetate, which we view against the printed page behind it. The torn mats are aged and distressed with brown ink. Small brass frames anchor a few of the mementos in place.

AN OUTSTRETCHED HAND

ALTERED BOOK | *Kim Smith*

*B*lack and antique metallic colors dominate this book cover. A corrugated cardboard open hand, highlighted with metallic gold, hangs by four small chains in the center of a rectangular window cut into the cover of the book. The remaining book cover is painted with a selection of metallic and black paint, and strong shapes are stamped over the background in heavy black ink. The cover is handsome, and the hand adds a curiously fascinating element. Dramatic thready fibers drape off the edge of one interior page, softening the hard edges of the book.

GARDEN

ALTERED BOOK | *Kim Smith*

A light summery page for a summer garden full of beautiful blooms and butterflies, including one that pops up as you open the page. Torn lightweight, colorful, printed paper rests atop the book pages bordered with pastel inks applied with a direct-to-paper technique. The paper violet and purples support the colors in the inked borders of the spread.

MONET'S GARDEN

HAND-PAINTED BACKGROUND PAGES | *Shelley Fuhr*

An exquisite oil-painted background—an impression of Monet's garden at Giverney —provides support for the panoramic photograph of the garden with the famous water lilies. The craft artist created these beautiful scrapbook pages in response to the fulfillment of a long-wished-for dream of visiting Monet's garden. Her facing page is a mosaic grid of geometric-shaped cropped garden photos, arranged in a pleasing pattern. Saturated color, rich texture, and organized images create a stunning scrapbook spread.

THE FUHR TREE

HAND-PAINTED BACKGROUND PAGES | *Shelley Fuhr*

An extraordinary family tree displayed on a sumptuous scenic garden painted background. One set of the parents' photographs are mounted inside simple decorative wooden frames, adding texture and depth to the page. The children's photographs lie flush with the painted background. The palette is sensitive and accents the colors in the clothing. On the facing page, the beautiful photograph of the three children together is featured, surrounded by journaling on transparent sheets that echo the shapes in the painted background.

EGG BASKET

QUILLED, DYED QUAIL EGGS | *Jan Williams*

*D*elicate quilled flowers and greenery embellish brilliant-colored, pigment-inked quail eggs—looking every bit like decorated Russian Easter eggs nestled in their basket. The blown eggs are first colored with pigment inks and then the quilled flowers and leaves are glued on to the dry eggs. Sumptuous colors, intricate paper filigree, and stunning textures contribute to the splendid effect. (See page 26.) Quilled paper coils can be affixed to any surface that will hold glue.

Basic Quilled Shapes

LOOSE GLUED COIL

Roll the paper on the quilling tool to form a coil. Remove the coil from the tool. Allow the coil to relax and expand to desired size, and apply a small amount of glue to the end of the paper strip, gluing down to the coil.

TIGHT COIL

Roll the paper on the quilling tool to form a coil. DO NOT allow the coil to relax and expand. While the coil is still on the tool, apply a small amount of glue to the end of paper strip, gluing down to the coil. Gently remove the coil from the tool.

TEARDROP

Make a loose glued coil. Pinch at one end of the coil to form a teardrop shape.

SHAPED TEARDROP

Make a teardrop. Run your fingernail toward the point curling the point in one direction.

SQUARE

HALF CIRCLE

Make a loose glued coil. Flatten the coil between your fingers. Hold the flattened coil upright between thumb and index finger with the points at the top and bottom. Flatten again matching up the previous two folds created by the points. Reopen to form a square shape.

Make a loose glued coil. Flatten one side of the coil by pinching the circle at two points or flatten the coil gently against your finger.

Quilling Shapes and Instructions by Jan Williams

Basic Quilled Shapes

TRIANGLE

Make a teardrop shape. Hold the teardrop at the pointed end between your thumb and index finger. Gently press the rounded end back until three points are formed.

Make a marquise. Run your fingernail toward one point curling it up. Repeat at the other end curling in the opposite direction.

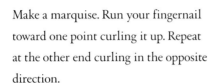

SHAPED MARQUISE

Make a loose glued coil. Pinch at the exact opposite side of the coil to form points at both ends, forming a marquise shape.

MARQUISE

Fold a piece of paper in half. Rolling toward the centerfold, roll each end of the paper in toward the centerfold.

OPEN HEART

Make a loose glued coil. Flatten the coil between your fingers. Hold the flattened coil upright between your thumb and index finger with points at the top and bottom. Slowly begin to flatten the coil once again moving the previous points slightly away from each other rather than matching them as in the square shape. Reopen to form a rectangle.

RECTANGLE

BUNNY EAR

Make a loose glued coil. Gently push the coil against the quilling tool (¼-inch diameter) to form a shape similar to the crescent, but with the two points closer together.

HOLLY LEAF

Make a loose glued coil, and flatten between your fingers. Hold the flattened coil in the center tightly with tweezers. Gently push one end toward the center with your index finger and thumb forming two more points. Repeat at opposite end. Reshape leaf as needed.

ROLLED HEART (ARROW)

Make a teardrop. Hold the teardrop shape between the thumb and index finger of one hand. Gently push the center of the rounded end back using the straight edge of the tweezers. Crease at both sides of the pushed-in end.

CRESCENT

Make a teardrop. Pinch one more point not quite opposite the first point. Run your fingernail toward both points curling the points up or make a loose glued coil. Press the coil against the rounded side of your quilling tool or finger to form a crescent.

"V" SHAPE

Fold the paper in half. Curl each end of paper away from centerfold forming semi-tight coils at each end.

Quilling Shapes and Instructions by Jan Williams

DECORATED GOOSE EGG

PUNCHED PAPER | *Jan Williams*

Lush punched flowers and greenery fall over the surface of a painted goose egg in an exquisite palette that is irresistible—soft blues, violets, and greens. The flower centers are folded and snipped, and the leaves are veined with a green pen. Undulating texture and soft color are the focus of this project.

A GARDEN OF DELIGHT

QUILLED OSTRICH EGG | *Jan Williams*

Not too many of us will attempt this quilled project (right). It is absolutely extraordinary. The artist told us that it took her four hours to carve the opening. We can only imagine the time it took for the cascading meadow of flowers with little yellow butterflies. You can look at this for hours on end. A sculpted base of florist's foam supports the rolling meadow. The soft palette of blue, green, and white is accented with two tiny spots of yellow (the butterflies). A stunning sculptural piece of graceful scrollwork, a long-respected paper art.

Fabric

We have always believed that what you can do with paper, you can do with fabric, and vice-versa. Paper crafters are intertwining paper and fabric in extraordinary ways. Like fabric, paper can be stitched, pierced, and woven. Embroidery, woven ribbons, lace, ribbons, rickrack, yarn-like fibers, and cut-and-torn fabric pieces can complement and enhance scrapbooks, cards, or other paper craft projects.

Do you have extra bits of fabric left over from another project? Attach them and use them as ribbons to decorate special gift packages. Make a card by cutting a shape out of cardboard and covering it with fabric. (See our fabric star card on page 79.) One ribbon bow on a project is lovely; a ribbon tied around a project with or without a bow is stunning; ribbon attaching another embellishment to a project is great. And try punching a shape out of cardstock—perhaps a flower shape—and running a patterned ribbon behind the negative shape on your card or page. Or create a gift album quickly by attaching individual tags or matted pages together with a bouquet of rich-colored organdy ribbons. One of our favorite projects is a woven-satin-ribbon background created for a scrapbook page. One artist has embroidered exquisite flowers from Monet's garden at Giverney on her scrapbook pages (page 76), remembering an extraordinary visit. The possibilities are many.

SPRING GARDEN

STAMPED CANVAS BAG | *Adrienne Kennedy*

A practical-yet-charming natural canvas bag stamped and bedecked with ribbons is perfect to bring into any garden—your own or the garden of a friend. Filled with spring bulbs and seeds and appropriate small gardening tools, this is an ideal gift for your favorite gardener (see page 54).

Creating the Project

1. Stamp garden-related words on a natural canvas bag using acrylic paint.

2. Stitch fibers in the upper-left corner of the bag in a starburst pattern. Attach a button and metal accent in the center.

3. Wind strips of fabric around the handles, covering completely. Leave extra fabric for a generous fringe.

TIP *Put a piece of cardboard inside the bag when stamping on canvas so the paints don't bleed through to the back.*

PICNIC

INVITATION | *Kim Smith*

I nvite all the neighbors to a summer picnic with this ingenious invitation. The red and yellow wavy lines of rickrack used to embellish the hot dog with ketchup and mustard look outlandish and good enough to eat at the same time.

Creating the Project

1. Place red-and-white striped paper over the front of the card. Crimp a white circle and adhere to the front of card, making a paper plate for the hot dog.

2. Stamp and cut out the hot dog and roll. Glue rickrack to the hot dog and attach to the "paper plate" with foam adhesive.

3. Stamp the text on white cardstock and trim to make labels, mounting them to the card at carefree angles with foam adhesive.

SHE'S GOT A WAY ABOUT HER

SCRAPBOOK | *Trish Turay*

$\mathcal{D}$elightful, "pure girl" photos set to the lyrics of a favorite song, obviously with love, fill the pages of this small scrapbook celebrating a treasured child. Patterned paper paired with ribbon and flower embellishments decorate the pages of this pretty pink album.

Creating the Project

1. Cut and layer mats beneath the photos and adhere to the pages.

2. Print the song lyrics out on plain white paper and cut into one-line panels.

3. Attach a deep-pink cardstock panel to the right side of the right-hand page as a mat for the journaled panel. Secure with two brads on either end.

4. Staple silk ribbon tabs to the top of the page. Other album pages are decorated at the sides and tops with more ribbon tabs, silk flowers, and brads.

FRIEND

CARD | *Becky Baack*

A card celebrating friendship is a handmade treasure anyone would enjoy. The colorful rickrack adds just the right texture and interest to the soft palette. The rickrack complements the stitching on the card.

Creating the Project

1. Cut paper to fit the front of the card. Tear another paper to make a pocket. Layer the smaller pocket-piece over the larger one from the left side of the paper. Zig-zag stitch with a sewing machine along the top and bottom of the paper, attaching it to the card. Machine stitch rickrack down the left side of the card.

2. Print an appropriate quote on vellum, handcolor, and back with more vellum. Stitch down the right side of the layered vellum. Tuck vellum into the pocket on the left side. Tear the right edge extending past the card.

MY DEAR HEART

CARD | *Kim Smith*

A small card, a quiet palette, and coordinated textures speak of gentleness and warmth. The card is simple, unassuming, and effective.

Creating the Project

1. Stamp text background onto a yellow silk flower.

2. Stamp a greeting on a small punched tag.

3. Attach the tag to the flower with a brad in the center, attaching to layered card-stock squares.

PRECIOUS DARLING

PHOTO FRAME | *Adrienne Kennedy*

A framed photo becomes a beautiful keepsake to adorn the wall of a house. The stamped photo mat adds depth and tone. Embellishments with coordinating ribbon and a silk flower add texture and a refreshing splash of color.

Creating the Project

1. Stamp the mat with word stamps using three synchronized colors. Stamp each word a second time before re-inking to vary the intensity of the color.

2. Tie a column of pink and white ribbons to the left side of the white frame. Attach a wide ribbon and a silk flower to the upper-right corner of the frame using a glue gun.

3. Add the photo to the frame.

FLOWER BASKET

CARD | *Kim Smith*

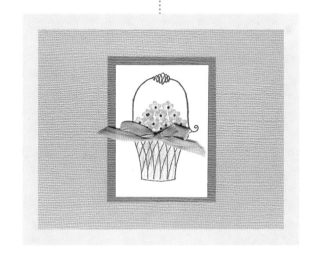

A flower-filled basket adorns this little note card. Embellished with a ribbon, this card can say Thanks, I miss you, or just Hello.

1. Stamp the basket on white cardstock with black ink and the flowers with purple ink.

2. Accent the centers of each flower with a glitter pen. Use colored pencil to color in the base of the basket.

3. Tie a ribbon bow and glue it at the top of the basket. Cut into a rectangle, mat and mount on the card.

BLOOM BABY BLOOM

SCRAPBOOK PAGE | *Stacey Turachek*

A baby discovering the joy of a garden in springtime is a pleasing sight. Stalks of green-and-white ribbon support the simple punched blossoms of pink, blue, and white cardstock. The background and decorative colors support those in the photographs.

Creating the Project

1. Cover the scrapbook page with printed, striped paper.

2. Punch six flower blooms, two each in three different sizes in three different colors.

3. Create the flower stems with green-and-white ribbon, tying a knot in a short ribbon piece to create leaves. Mat two photographs on white cardstock and place on the page at opposite corners.

AUTUMN

TAG | *Michelle Tardie*

The warm colors and dusty feel of this well-worn-looking tag make us sense the end of summer. Use this tag to embellish a layout or attach to a "farewell to summer" gift basket.

Creating the Project

1. Cover the tag with patterned paper and top with pieces of magic mesh. Add walnut ink over the surface.

2. Cut "autumn" die-cut to fit and attach to the tag with foam adhesive. Rub walnut ink onto the flowers and attach to the tag with a brad.

3. Cut the cardstock tag slightly larger than the tag and adhere together with foam adhesive. Tie the cord around the bottom of the tag and fibers through the top hole.

SIX MONTHS

TAG | *Michelle Tardie*

What a sweet way to remember the delight of seeing your baby's development. Adorn this charming tag with a fabric flower (complete with a summertime busy bee) and a bow. The palette is pleasing and consistent.

Creating the Project

1. Cover the front of a tag with soft-green ribbed cardstock.

2. Use metallic rub-ons around the edges of the covered tag and on the flower. Center a rectangle of patterned paper on the covered tag. leaving a border of ribbed green cardstock top and bottom.

3. Print the appropriate words on clear acetate. Trim and adhere the acetate to the tag with brads in a coordinated color. Add a small text block with foam adhesive.

4. Attach a flower with a brad in the center, and glue on the butterfly. Tie the top of the tag with coordinated ribbon.

HALLOWEEN

METALLIC CHARM CARD | *Kim Smith*

Woven ribbon in Halloween colors provides a textured background for a ghostly Halloween brad. Use it to invite your friends over for cocoa on this spooky night. The small image on a sea of brown cardstock is clean and powerful.

Creating the Project

1. Cut a window opening in the card front and surround the back of the opening with adhesive.

2. Weave the ribbons, starting in the center and working out to the edges. Attach the woven ribbon panel behind the window opening.

3. Back the inside front of the card with matching brown cardstock to cover the ribbon ends.

4. Insert the brad through the ribbons and cardstock.

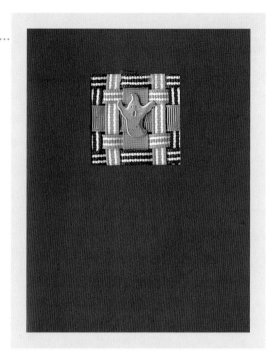

TIP *Use the tip of a craft knife to create a slit for easy insertion of the brads.*

THINKING OF YOU

FABRIC-PANEL CARD | *Rachael Giallongo*

Basic shapes and antiqued edges add style to this handsome, masculine all-occasion card suitable for a man in your life—husband, sweetheart, father, brother.

Creating the Project:

1. Rub black ink around the edges on the front of a textured mahogany-brown card.

2. Attach a wide band of fabric to the card bottom with glue dots.

3. Arrange alphabet stickers to spell "Thinking" on the card above the fabric.

4. Attach alphabet brads through the fabric and cardstock.

5. Attach a folded accent ribbon with a staple.

HOLIDAY JOY

CARD | *Adrienne Kennedy*

The old-fashioned look of the rubber-stamped text pairs with the antique patterned paper on this holiday card. A red-and-green checked ribbon adds appropriate texture and light to this retro card.

Creating the Project

1. Cover the bottom three inches of the card with seasonal patterned paper.

2. Stamp the sentiment centered horizontally near the top of the card.

3. Punch two holes just above the patterned paper and tie a ribbon through the holes.

A HEART FULL OF THANKS

CARD | *Kim Smith*

The message of this little card is repeated inside and outside the punched heart shape. The repetition on the twill tape seals the thought.

Creating the Project

1. Punch a heart shape in the center of the card front.

2. Stamp the red cardstock repeatedly with a background stamp of "Thanks" and "Thank you" using white ink. Attach stamped cardstock behind the heart opening.

3. Use brads to attach printed twill tape across the punched heart shape.

4. Back the inside front cover of the card with matching brown cardstock cut to fit.

FRIENDSHIP

CARD | *Rachael Giallongo*

THE ONLY WAY TO HAVE A FRIEND IS TO BE ONE.
Ralph Waldo Emerson

TIP *If paper warps after being painted and dried, iron on the back side until flat, using a medium setting.*

This lovely card has been aged and distressed to soften its look. The strong, straightforward quote from Ralph Waldo Emerson sends a good message. The delicate palette and motif bring the message into an immediate context.

Creating the Project

1. Cut patterned paper to fit the front of the card. Crumple, and then sand the paper.

2. Create a whitewash with acrylic paint and water and paint the surface of the paper and the flowers. Let dry completely.

3. Attach decorative brads to the center of the three flowers and adhere to the card.

4. Machine-stitch the dry printed paper to the card. Add the sticker quote.

PARKER

DIMENSIONAL KEEPSAKE HOLDER ALBUM | *Jamie Kilmartin*

A small gift album featuring charming beach photos of Parker with his cousin MacKenzie on a family vacation. The laminated pages of the album mean they withstand many hours of sandy hands sorting through them. The decorative red rickrack colorfully disguises the seam of the acetate window on the keepsake holder cover.

Creating the Project

1. Add the perfect photograph and a collection of shells to the keepsake holder. Add red rickrack over the seam where the window attaches to the cover.

2. Determine how many pages you would like. Crop photos, decorate as desired, and mount on red, yellow, or blue mats.

3. Laminate the matted photos back-to-back. Punch a hole at top left of laminated pages. Attach a metal ring/clip to hold the album together, a bouquet of ribbons, and a name tag.

LIAM AT TWO

GIFT ALBUM | *Marla Kress*

A small (2 ¾-inch) square gift album of informal close-up portraits, a perfect combination of journaling and photos, for grandmother's purse or for Dad to carry with him on a business trip. This project of parents appreciating their disarming, expressive little boy being a little boy is a gift to keep forever.

Creating the Project

1. Crop six close-up photos to 2 ¾ inches square. Using an awl, or a pin, scratch a natural built-in frame just inside the edges of the photos.

2. Create collage pages for the backs of the photos with decorative sticker letters and text printed from your computer mounted on various printed papers.

3. Embellish the journaled pages as you wish.

4. Punch a hole in each leaf and attach to a large metal ring. Add the titling labels.

ALL ABOUT ME

SCRAPBOOK ALBUM | *Trish Turay*

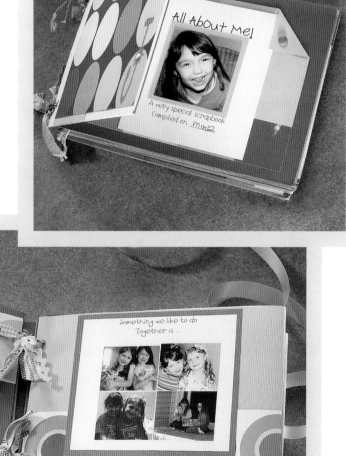

An absolutely delightful personal album a little girl will cherish for years to come. This is an intimate way to relish the precocious kindergarten age: school-age children can write in their own handwriting all about their favorite things to do, and the things that make them happy. The two-ring-binder layout makes it easy for children to read it themselves, time and again. Think about creating the pages for a friend or relative, or for your own child to complete on his or her own, or with your help!

Creating the Project

1. Create the album cover by punching two holes on one edge of 8 ½ x 6-inch chipboard and layer with printed paper and appropriate embellishments.

2. Use the same size cardstock for the inside pages. Decorate with a combination of plain and patterned papers and photographs with coordinated color mats, leaving room for the child's journaling.

10 REASONS WHY I LOVE YOU

POCKET ALBUM | *Trish Turay*

*T*here are few simpler ways to reinforce feelings of love for your special Valentine than this quick-and-easy pocket album. Tags are embellished to hold ten sentiments for your loved one. Print the reasons you are in love, mount one on a tag with a photo, slip each one into a pocket envelope, and bind the envelopes together with ribbon.

Creating the Project

1. Punch three holes along the side of each envelope and set eyelets in each hole. Tie the envelopes together using ribbon.

2. Rub the surface and edges of each tag with an inkpad. Decorate each tag by layering a variety of cut or torn decorative papers, a photo, a printed sentiment, and a ribbon.

3. Tear and ink decorative paper and adhere to the cover. Add text printed on cardstock, sticker letters, and a rub-on sentiment. Stamp with a date stamp.

MOMENTS OF NOSTALGIA

POSTCARD ALBUM | *Michelle Tardie*   **GIFT ALBUM** | *Adrienne Kennedy*

Capture all the memories of your travels in a small album with pockets designed to hold postcard mementos. Antique correspondence stickers on the cover give an indication of this album's purpose. The greyboard cover of a small wire-ring album is antiqued and stamped with an all-over background stamp in brown ink. A luscious dew-moistened dusty pink rose is framed with a small wood frame antiqued with brown ink. The brown and white ribbon anchors the frame and our attention to the cover. The muted palette is attractive and effective.

TWIN BEAUTIES

SCRAPBOOK PAGE | *Pam Klassen*

Why stop with embellishing the scrapbooking page? Decorate the photos themselves to add three-dimensional, unexpected fun to the layout. Elegant and glamorous decorations include beads, fur, and glitter, or a more playful tone can be set with mini buttons, funky fibers, and decorative brads. Adding color to a black-and-white image using chalks or inks is another way to brighten up a photo. In this heritage photo we have no way of knowing what color they were wearing, but isn't it fun to imagine?

Creating the Project

1. Enlarge and mount a matted photo on a background page. Tear patterned paper and attach below the photo. Cover the edges of the photo and paper with border stickers. Stamp the title and text on the page and photo.

2. Tea-dye white lace and color slightly with chalk. Adhere lace, faux fur, silk flowers, pearls, and rhinestones to the photo.

3. Apply dots of glitter glue to the hair and punched transparency stars to the background. Use dimensional paint to highlight the decoration on the photo mat.

4. Add sticker tags in the upper corner and attach fabric print with strips of stickers in the lower corner.

 TIP *Always make sure you have an additional copy of the photo before embellishing a photo in a layout.*

GOOD CHEER

CARDS AND GIFT PACKAGE | *Great American Stamp Store Artists*

*B*efore you start to create a card or gift package, think about the palette and composition. What colors will carry the message you want to send and elicit the response you want? Start with a simple card and add one or two decorative elements in appropriate, pleasing colors, with a dramatic composition and you will have created something lovely. These projects offer pleasing, unified palettes, interesting techniques, and simple, strong compositions. A small white, cushion box holds a punched-and-layered adornment in a centered composition. The soft blue and green woven paper heart is actually two cardstock tags cut and interwoven, creating a checkerboard effect. The next two cards relate to each other with reversed arrangements of the same colors and techniques: a letter template is colored and layered over a beribboned background. The final card, an invitation, offers a display of three different-sized fabric flowers held together with green ribbons.

BITS OF NATURE

TAGGED CARD | *Jackie Hull*

$\mathcal{A}$ stunning dark blue-green, lightly textured card provides a dramatic background for three decorated white tags wrapped with different fibers displayed across its center. Embellishments include buttons, a silk flower with a long twirled stem, several kinds of ribbons (each tag has at least one ribbon), a tiny glass jar, a journaling panel, a seashell, and glittery fiber. The color is strong, the textures intriguing. The designer makes good use of leftover scraps.

MEMORIES

TRIO OF CARDS| *Jackie Hull*

$\mathcal{W}$e all search for connections, and looking to old photos and memorabilia helps us find those connections. It proves that, after all, we are nostalgic creatures. Seeing what was in the past helps us to understand the present, and perhaps prepare for the future. This trio of cards is full of nostalgia, from old photos, white lace, ornamental photo corners and deckle-edged mats and borders, to an old-fashioned muted palette.

TWO

SCRAPBOOK | *Sherry Cartwright*

"Tell me what I was like at two," any parent of a four-year-old will hear often. This layout is dedicated to remembering favorite things and special moments. Stamped fabric tabs spell out the age, and then just undo the button to read creative journaling hidden beneath the photo. What a lovely way to let a toddler know how much he is cherished!

Creating the Project

1. Tear the top and bottom edges of white cardstock and adhere to a blue "denim" background page.

2. Layer the transparency printed with "cherish" text on the left edge of a large mat of red cardstock and adhere with a strip of blue paper woven through a D-ring.

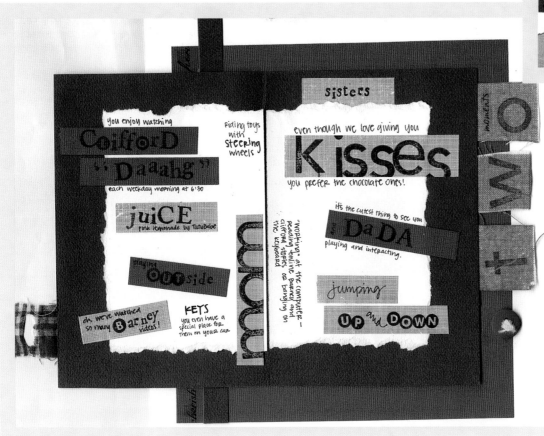

3. Create a card and mount a photo on top, adding a fabric tab with a hole for a button. Layer this to the page as shown with cut fabric tabs peeking out from behind.

4. Stamp on fabric tabs and sew a button to the page as a closure for the card.

5. Add stamped and printed journaling on white mats inside the card.

GIFT BOX

FABRIC RIBBON AND TAG | *Becky Baack*

Wondering what to do with extra bits of fabric? Use them in place of ribbon to decorate special gift packages. The stamped paper provides a natural stage for a dramatic burst of color and texture. The fabric has been sewn onto paper, and paper has been sewn onto a fabric tag so you can address the package.

Creating the Project

1. Stamp wrapping paper, let dry, and wrap the gift.

2. Stack four pieces of 1 ³/₄-inch-wide coordinating fabrics long enough to wrap around the package on a strip of slightly narrower thin paper.

3. Machine-stitch down the center of all thicknesses.

4. Fringe fabric strips by cutting in toward the center through all layers every ³/₄ inch.

5. Create a ³/₈-inch fabric center strip by repeating step 3. Adhere around the package with double-sided tape.

6. Sew a paper tag to fabric, fray the edges, and tie to the package with rickrack.

HINT: *Make several of these ahead of time for easy gift-giving embellishments.*

TIP *As the fabric ribbon is handled it will continue to fray and fluff. This is a good thing!*

REMEMBER

WOVEN RIBBON SCRAPBOOK PAGE | *Stacey Turachek*

An exquisite woven white satin ribbon background sets an elegant tone for the photos of a delightful baby girl. The simple palette keeps the photos and textured decorative elements in focus. The photos are framed with pink mats and layered with decorative white ribbons. The woven background of $^1/_2$-inch white satin ribbon is framed with white velvet ribbon and clear acrylic photo corners. The large photo lifts on the hinges to reveal an appropriate quote. A small metal frame holds the minimal journaling.

MONET'S GARDEN

EMBROIDERED SCRAPBOOK PAGES | *Shelley Fuhr*

*T*his strikingly elegant layout draws us right into Monet's garden outside of Paris with beautiful ribbon-embroidered flowers. The century-old ribbon-craft technique used on these pages uses narrow ribbon in the same way as embroidery thread to create a gorgeous bouquet of flowers. If this ribbon craft looks too daunting to you, try a simple embellishment of two or three flowers to embellish a photo mat or tag.

Creating the Project

1. Cut photos and adhere across the page. Use illustrations below as a guide to create stitched flowers with ribbon.

2. Stitch sequin, pearl, and bead accents to the centers of various flowers.

3. On the journaled page, coil a pattern of fibers randomly around the page as a border. Hand-stitch fibers in place. Add embroidered ribbon flowers along the border.

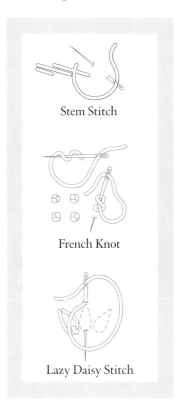

Stem Stitch

French Knot

Lazy Daisy Stitch

TIP *Use a tapestry needle that will make a hole large enough for the ribbon to pass through your paper, and with an eye large enough to accommodate the width of the ribbon.*

MY LOVE "FUHR" LIFE RUNS IN THE FAMILY

EMBROIDERED SCRAPBOOK PAGES | *Shelley Fuhr*

These sumptuous scrapbook pages are created by an artist who brings her work in paint, ribbon embroidery, and dress design to her dramatic, dimensional album pages. She is unafraid to use a wide variety of materials to adorn her work. The results are truly fantastic! The lacy effect of the bustier mounted on black cardstock on the left side of the page is created with ribbon ironed on to the lavender patterned paper. The black tulle gown, the artist's own design, is hand-embroidered with silk ribbons. The dress was sketched out on paper first, then made with fabric, and embroidered. With the second page the artist celebrates the creative talents of her family. Fabric and paper flowers adorn the layered photos. The column of small photos on the right are elevated from the page with mounting tape.

PLUM SUEDE

ACCORDION BOOK | *Christine Timmons*

An elegant accordion gift book covered in sophisticated plum suede is embellished simply with a small rectangle of printed fabric and tied with a narrow deep-turquoise ribbon. The palette continues on the interior pages collaged with a mixed-media world of tumbling whole and partial geometric shapes, layered fabric and paper scraps, stamped handwriting, stitching, thread, snaps, and stamps from faraway places. Machine-stitched paths and bridges of turquoise tie the journey together.

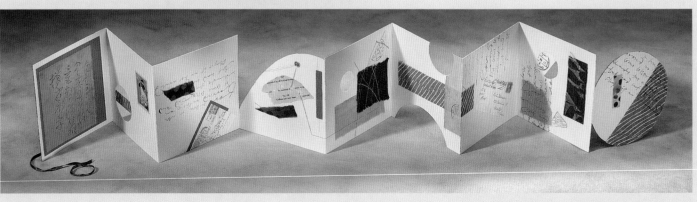

MIXED-MEDIA TRIO

COLLAGED CARDS | *Christine Timmons*

*S*hape, line, and texture are the focus with these projects. A star-shaped card covered in fabric, another folded at a forty-five-degree angle and fastened with a silk ribbon loop, and a snippet from an end-of-the-bolt imported silk fabric are featured on these cards. The unifying element with this group is the use of fabric and paper together—each card offers a different texture and shape. Hand- and machine-sewing, torn edges of a paper panel, and a silk cord layered on fabric mats of contrasting texture create imaginative dimension.

Glass and Plastic

Dress up your paper crafts with jewels of glass and plastic. Add sparkle and glitter with glass, adhesive or liquid beads and mosaic mirrors, decorative acrylic buttons, tiles, and frames, and tiny acrylic message tags ready to be painted. You'll be delighted with the range of materials available to you.

And don't forget the finishing materials like diamond glaze or MicaMagic™. Remember shrink plastic, or try creating a design on a sheet of transparency. It is the understated small details that help you raise your projects to new creative heights. And sometimes that is nothing more than a tiny jewel placed at the center of a die-cut flower, or a dab or two of a glistening liquid, or even a watch fob placed over an image. And have you wondered what to do with all those extra buttons you have saved? A border of pretty buttons is a delightful addition to a scrapbook page or box. A favorite project of ours is a soft painted frame with a tiny glass bottle containing quartz crystals accenting the frame palette.

The most important thing to remember is that you decide what to use on your craft projects, and you have an extraordinary number of glass and plastic materials from which to choose. The bits of glass beads, flowers, pebbles, jewels add gloss and dimension to every paper craft project.

MY HEART'S TREASURE

ALBUM | *Pam Klassen*

*B*rightly decorated with small round mirrors that reflect the design of the patterned paper, this useful little album with a purse handle is easy to tote around. It waits for anyone who wants to take a look at the treasures that are hidden inside.

Creating the Project

1. Remove the front cover of the album and cover with patterned paper. Punch holes for the wire binding.

2. Apply a large rub-on monogram and stamp additional letters. Stamp on an oval mirror and glue seven round mirrors inside the circles of the patterned paper.

3. Tie a purchased purse handle to the spiral binding with ribbon. Tie on additional ribbons and staple ribbons to the page tops, so they can peek out of the album.

FAVORITE SUMMERTIME RECIPES

FOLDED PAPER BAG POCKET ALBUM | *Trish Turay*

Need a gift for friends moving away? How about a collection of recipes (and perhaps some memories) gathered from times together? Folded brown-paper lunch bags are stapled together back-to-back inside the album. Each pocket holds a decorated recipe card. Folded ribbons stapled to the inside pockets add a fringe-like finish. The homespun, old-fashioned, well-loved, red-checked tablecloth cover sets the right tone. Buttons, a giant painted initial letter, and cooking-utensil stickers decorate the simple title panels.

DRAGONFLY

ACRYLIC FRAME CARD | *Jan Williams*

A quilled bright raspberry dragonfly is surrounded by a clear acrylic frame. Colorful patterned paper behind the frame adjusts the color to fit the palette of any project you create.

Creating the Project

1. Stamp a dragonfly in the center of a small piece of white cardstock.

2. Quill teardrop shapes to create the dimensional dragonfly. Glue the quilled dragonfly to the stamped one at an angle, slightly off-center of the stamped image to create interesting texture and shadow.

3. Attach the cardstock to the back of a clear acrylic frame. Back the acrylic frame with patterned paper. Cut two narrow strips of the same patterned paper and attach to the card on an angle, as shown.

A HAPPY BIRTHDAY

ACRYLIC FRAME | *Adrienne Kennedy*

A clear acrylic frame highlights the initial monogram. The palette is basic black-and-white with interesting patterned papers, the clear frame, a simple ribbon, and an eye-catching off-center placement of the focal point.

Creating the Project

1. Layer two patterned papers and glue to the front of the card.

2. Stamp the "Happy Birthday" message in the lower corner and the "A" off-center at the left of the card.

3. Wrap the ribbon around the card and tie it to the acrylic frame around the decorative initial "A."

HOLIDAY CHEER

CARD WITH PLASTIC CHARM | *Kim Smith*

*S*imple texture and simple color work together to present this delightful little plastic charm purchased commercially. The red-and-green polka-dot ribbon ties it all together. An easy card to make, with an effective, simple embellishment.

Creating the Project

1. Cut a narrow piece of red cardstock.

2. Pull a piece of red-and-green polka-dot ribbon through the loop of the charm and glue onto the top center of the red cardstock. Tie a bow with the same ribbon and glue it onto the top of the ribbon loop holding the charm.

3. Stamp the holiday message near the bottom center of the red cardstock strip, and glue it to the center of the green card.

A TOUCH OF COLOR

FRAME WITH MAHJONG TILES | *Kim Smith*

A tumble of Mahjong tiles pair with Asian stamps to create a warm frame for a photograph of a charming toddler. The simple frame palette is complemented by the small bright-colored tiles, echoing the colors in the baby's clothing. Small canvas frames are lovely gifts, either decorated or left for the recipient to decorate.

Creating the Project

1. Ink the surface of the canvas frame with a direct-to-canvas technique and stamp the series of Asian images at an angle across the surface.

2. Glue the tiles at an angle to the upper-right corner of the frame.

CELEBRATE FAMILY

GIFT ALBUM | *Marla Kress*

A flutter of ribbons attached to small plastic tags with family-friendly messages reach from every page of this charming small album of family memories. Each miniature scrapbook page is independent, making it easy for you to change the order of the pages as you wish. Ribbons, stitching, and patterned papers, acrylic tags and journaling panels embellish the engaging pages.

Creating the Project

1. Print the text out from your computer and trim to basic geometric shapes, or purchase commercial die-cut message panels. Gather a selection of patterned papers.

2. Place patterned papers and photographs cropped to size on the album pages.

3. Add the journaling panels.

4. Attach acrylic message tags to the pages with brads. Tie a ribbon through the end of each tag.

5. Decorate the cover with an acrylic frame and tag.

CHEERS!

COLORED ACRYLIC ATTACHMENTS | *Marla Kress*

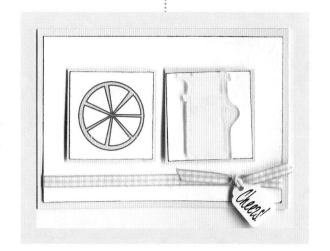

This bright sunshiny card does exactly as intended, instantly cheering you up! Adding color to acrylic embellishments gives a bright kick of color.

Creating the Project

1. Cut yellow cardstock to create a 4 x 6-inch card. Cut white cardstock slightly smaller than the yellow card front. Wrap the white cardstock panel with yellow gingham ribbon, ink the edges, and adhere to the yellow card.

2. Print the lemon from clip art. Cut squares of yellow cardstock; and then cut slightly smaller squares of white cardstock. Ink the edges of the white squares.

3. Accent acrylic embellishment with yellow paint, wiping off the excess. Color the white square mat beneath the pitcher with yellow chalk. Attach the colored acrylic pitcher to the chalked square.

4. Attach the squares to the card with foam adhesive and tie the tag to the ribbon.

FLOWERS 3

PLASTIC FLOWER BUTTONS | *Kim Smith*

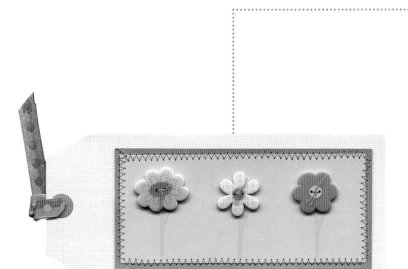

Bright springtime flowers embellish a pretty tag just waiting to be passed on to bring cheer and good wishes to a special friend.

Creating the Project

1. Machine-stitch together two cardstock mats (one pink, one blue) using a zig-zag stitch.

2. Stamp stems evenly spaced across the front of the blue mat.

3. Select three flower buttons. Tie thread through the buttonholes and glue the buttons to the card at the tops of the stamped stems.

4. Attach the mat to the tag. Add punched reinforcement to the hole and finish with ribbon.

FLOWER IN A BOTTLE

CARD WITH DIAMOND GLAZE | *Kim Smith*

A pretty little note that says "I am thinking of you." The understated, elegant simplicity of this card makes the surprise of the shiny glass bottle holding the flower and the subtle color and texture of the flower all the more surprising. The added glaze brings the stamped elements to life. The off-center placement of the components promotes a feeling of motion and energy.

Creating the Project

1. Create a 3 ½ x 5-inch card from lightly textured blue cardstock. Add the coordinated ribbon border near the front edge of the card.

2. Stamp the image in black ink, and color with colored pencil.

3. Cover the bottle with clear diamond glaze and the flower center with liquid pearl.

4. Trim the image to a small panel, cut light-blue cardstock for a shadow mat, and mount to the card.

TIP *Clear glaze will add a shiny glass finish to any surface it covers.*

SWIM

MOSAIC TILES | *Rachael Giallongo*

M osaic tiles in three shades of blue in a column down the side of the card add texture, dimension, and even sophistication to a water-filled card. The focal point of this tag in a beautifully coordinated palette is the young swimmer. A moment captured thoughtfully.

Creating the Project

1. Cut patterned paper, cardstock, and photo into a tag shape. Ink the edges of the patterned paper. Trim the photo to allow for the addition of five tiles. Mount the photo to cardstock, cardstock to patterned paper, and tiles to cardstock.

2. Add the tiles, and the rub-on letters. Punch a hole and add an eyelet.

OUR DOG

SCRAPBOOK PAGE | *Rachael Giallongo*

Don't forget the most dedicated family member and friend. Our dogs deserve their own scrapbook pages, and much more. Celebrate the family dog's affection and loyalty with style. This page features a lovely portrait and decorative acrylic word-charm panels with dog-related copy. The blue paint on the clear charms emphasizes the text. Duchess's leash is at the ready.

Creating the Project:

1. Mask off a 3 x 6-inch rectangle on a red background page (to create a clear space for the acrylic word charms) and stamp with a texture stamp. Remove the mask.

2. Paint acrylic word charms with acrylic paint. Allow to dry for three to five minutes. Wipe away excess paint, leaving the paint only in the incised words.

3. Paint chipboard letters with blue paint, then with crackle medium, and then with red paint. Allow to dry between each coat.

4. Attach the acrylic word charms to the page over the masked area, using twine and glue dots.

5. Add sticker letters and tag. Wrap polka-dot ribbon across the page, attaching it on the back.

ADORED AND LOVED

ACRYLIC LETTER SCRAPBOOK PAGE | *Rachael Giallongo*

Celebrate a child simply for being a child, and for the process of growing up. The small, everyday life moments are touching, and help our children realize that we don't love them because they excel in one thing or another. We love and adore them just because they are themselves. A large photo of a lovely young girl is matted with soft colors and glued to the 8 x 8-inch page. A matted journaling panel and a great big acrylic initial highlighted with pigment ink tied onto the page with rickrack add a delicate touch.

BUTTERFLY

CARD WITH ACRYLIC BUTTON | *Dave Brethauer*

*T*here are so many products to choose from, and this wonderfully understated card makes good use of some available materials. The stamped image is elegantly simple in lovely colors that have been enhanced with colored pencil. The flowers on the tree are brads, and the butterfly is an acrylic Doodlebug button. The butterfly path has been stitched with machine sewing. All of the embellishments are added to the white cardstock panel before mounting it onto the blue card.

Creating the Project

1. Cut a white cardstock panel slightly smaller than the blue card.

2. Stamp the tree in the center of the white panel and machine-stitch a wavy path across the tree.

3. Attach flower brads to the tree and glue an acrylic button at the end of the stitched path.

4. Attach the white panel to the card front.

FLOWERS IN VASE

CARD WITH PUNCHED VELLUM | *Karen Gerbrandt*

A combination of delicate pen work and punched vellum shapes gives this dimensional card a light feeling. The palette is pleasing, the textures and flower arrangement exquisitely delicate, and the off-center composition intriguing.

Creating the Project

1. Punch flower shapes from blue vellum. Place shapes on craft foam and push the centers with the rounded end of a pen, pressing firmly, until flowers curl. Glue rhinestones in the flower centers. For buds cut two petals from a flower and fold in half.

2. Cut a rectangle from crinkled cardstock for the vase and tie with gold cord. Adhere the vase to the card. Hand-draw the branched stems with green ink, and use a stipple technique to create ferns. Glue flowers to the ends of the stems.

VINTAGE ROMANCE

BUTTONS, FABRIC FLOWERS, AND LACE | *Jackie Hull*

Gentle colors, consistent palettes, and vintage bits combine to give us reflective moments of love and romance from an earlier time. Did earlier generations have more time? Did they take more pleasure in assembling the materials of their existence—*that* bit of lace, *that* particular button, *that* fabric flower—all of which had special meaning and were saved for the perfect moment? This duet is a love song with layers and textures and soft rhythms. The imaginative use of glass slides focuses our attention.

TIME PAST

GLASS NUGGET CARDS | *Jackie Hull*

Shapes, dimension, and texture! Layered shapes cut from an old Romance novel, printed paper, and plain paper, glass jewels, pewter buckles, giant glass nuggets, lace, and a jewel-studded crown—fantasy galore. The gold glitter over the cameo tag (the portrait with subtly colored lips) on the right adds a regal touch. The small crown balanced on the large head of the cut-out figure on the left is wonderfully whimsical.

SWEET GIRL

BUTTONED-UP SCRAPBOOK PAGE | *Sherry Cartwright*

Who can resist a picture of a baby sleeping? A perfect moment to treasure and preserve. And what to do with all those leftover buttons? They make a fine border of garden flowers surrounding the sleeping child's photo.

Creating the Project

1. Layer a piece of striped paper down the right side of the background page. Cut a square from patterned paper, cutting around the lower circle. Accent sticker letters and paper text with pens.

2. Cut a photo mat slightly larger than your photo. With a decorative scissors trim along the bottom edge of the mat. Punch a row of holes just above the decorative bottom edge to accent the cut. Mount the photo using photo corners.

3. Attach button embellishments to the page with glossy adhesive, adding silk flowers and tying on a mini tag.

FLOWER BOUQUET

SHRINK-PLASTIC DECORATION | *Heather Boling*

A fabulous way to maximize the use of your one-size stamp images. Stamp a simple flower design and leaf in three colors on a shrink plastic sheet. Cut and shrink it, and you have a new size, a new dimension, and a new texture. Let your imagination take hold.

Creating the Project

1. Stamp the flower image on shrink plastic several times each in red and in yellow, and stamp the leaf shape several times in green.

2. Silhouette the stamped flowers and leaf images. Follow the manufacturer's directions to shrink the plastic shapes.

3. Add color to the back of the shapes with paint pens. Draw outlines on the front of the pieces with a black pen made to be used on slick surfaces.

4. Wrap the box with raffia, and cut off the ends. Attach flowers to the box top using foam adhesive. Tie a gift tag to the package with raffia.

DREAM

SMALL DECORATIVE FRAME | *Sherry Cartwright*

*D*ream—of places far away, unknown, places you want to see. Or just let your mind wander and dream of anything that suits your fancy. Two small (5 x 5-inch) frames are covered with printed paper in tones of soft purples with warm accents, creating a sensitive, thoughtful mood, perfect for dreaming. The frames are mounted one on top of the other with foam mounting tape. The tiny glass bottle filled with quartz (or are they dreams?) rests in a hole cut for it in the top frame.

Creating the Project

1. Cover two frames with patterned paper.

2. Using a craft knife, cut a hole in the shape of a bottle to hold the bottle in the top frame. Tie the bottle and polka-dot ribbon to the frame. Add the acrylic word tag.

3. Fill the opening in the bottom frame with a photo and cover the back with paper. Attach the frames together with foam adhesive.

CELEBRATE

TIN-CAN LID WITH MICRO
GLASS BEADS | *Pam Klassen*

*A*n ingenious ornament, proving that you can use almost anything to embellish. Follow the steps below to embellish the tin-can lid with a sticker and glass beads.

Creating the Project

1. Cut patterned paper to fit inside the lid and adhere. Apply a butterfly sticker, cutting to fit within the lid. Add the "Celebrate" sticker.

2. Cut double-sided adhesive to fit inside the lid, apply tape over the paper and stickers.

3. Peel the backing off the tape and apply beads to cover the entire inside of the lid.

4. Cover the metal rim with double-sided tape. Remove backing from the tape and roll in the glitter/bead mixture.

5. Drill three small holes at the top and bottom of the lid. Wrap wire through the bottom, stringing beads and curling at the bottom.

6. Thread ribbon through the holes on the top and tie together forming a loop.

 Use this simple technique on almost any surface over any image to soften and magnify.

NOTES

BEADED NOTEPAD COVER | *Heather Boling*

"*A* bowl full of cherries" has spilled across this pretty little notepad cover. Made with sparkly self-adhesive beads and stamps, this easy project makes gift-giving a snap. The inked edges frame the front cover and draw us to the focal point of the clusters of tiny red-bead cherries.

Creating the Project

1. Ink the edges and corners of the notepad cover.

2. Adhere mounds of mostly red self-adhesive beads in pairs on the cover.

3. Draw stems and glue leaves at the tops. Stamp the text on the cover.

HEART OF FLOWERS

STITCHED SHOPPING BAG | *Kortney Langley*

A plain brown shopping bag becomes an inviting, personalized gift wrap for the lucky recipient.

Creating the Project

1. Cut out a denim heart with decorative-edged scissors and zig-zag stitch with a sewing machine around the outside edge.

2. Sew fabric flower shapes to the denim heart using random stitching patterns.

3. Sew on the buttons.

4. Hand-stitch stems onto the bag using an embroidery needle and thread. Tie ribbon to the stems and glue in their curled shapes.

5. Attach the decorated heart to the bag just above the embroidered stems.

SUNFLOWER

GIFT BOX WITH LIQUID BEADS | *Patti Behan*

A one-of-a-kind-looking gift box that can be used over and over again. The process can be applied to any size or style of lidded box.

Creating the Project

1. Spray paint a small 4 x 4-inch papier-mâché box and lid dark green.

2. Center a yellow fabric daisy on the top, and attach with glue.

3. Mound liquid beads in the center of the yellow daisy.

TIES THAT BIND

FAMILY ALBUM | *Patricia Milazzo*

This loving tribute to cherished grandparents has found a unique home in a tin CD case that is embellished to the nines! The use of black-and-white photos gives this sentimental package an ageless quality. Plastic embellishments include a frame along with word- and letter-tiles. A wonderful photo folder designed to fit perfectly in this tin holds memories that will be cherished for generations.

Creating the Project

1. Paint the CD tin. Cut patterned paper to fit front, back, and inside of the tin, inking all the edges.

2. Use acrylic paint to accent the acrylic frame and text tag, wiping off the excess. Back both pieces with patterned paper.

3. Ink the edges of the sticker word, cover with glaze and let dry. Adhere tile letters, sticker, acrylic text tag, and flowers to frame. Back the frame with the photo and mount onto the tin over the printed twill tape.

 Brush acrylic items with paint, let dry. Then lightly ink and set with a heat gun or spray with acrylic sealer.

KITTEN

EMBELLISHED PICTURE FRAME | *Nathalie Métivier for Magenta*

*M*agenta artists and materials are so elegant and refined their projects always look glorious. This embellished picture frame combines an appealing palette, texture, and a classic composition to great effect. The colors in the frames echo shades found in the photograph. And the textures complement what we see in the photo. It is the build-up of many layers of color that adds the depth and sophistication to the frame.

Creating the Project

1. Cover two foam frames (one 4³/₄-inch square and one 6-inch square) with several layers of fluid-chalk ink, the smaller frame mostly in peach and mauve tones, then stamped with patterns (no longer visible), and enhanced with black and green colored pencils and green Cat's Eyes™ and finally the little flower stamped with Copper MicaMagic™. Copper and bronze MicaMagic™ and little touches of green and lime gloss on top of several layers of fluid chalk-ink are the finishing touches on the larger frame.

2. Thread glass beads onto thin copper wire. Wrap the wire around the smaller frame with the beads resting on the front and sides of the frame.

3. Create a large outline flower with copper wire and attach to the bottom-left corner of the smaller frame. Attach an aluminum flower to the wire outline flower with a glue dot.

4. Tape the photo to the front of the larger frame. Attach the two frames together with glue dots (to allow for the copper wire wrapped around the front frame).

5. Add dots of glaze pen to accent the flower centers and to create a small triple-dot pattern.

TIP *Insert the copper wire into the foam to hide the ends of the wire. It is not difficult.*

THANKS

TRANSPARENCY CARD | *Pam Klassen*

A series of three layers of coordinating warm colors provide a perfect background for black stamped outline leaf shapes. The shimmering surface of the transparency adds drama. Follow the steps below to stamp and color the transparency.

Creating the Project

1. Ink the leaf stamp, then place an appropriate mask directly onto the rubber stamp before stamping on the rough side of the transparency.

2. Stamp the image again, on paper, and cut out random leaves. Use temporary adhesive to mask the same leaves on the stamped transparency images.

3. Ink a brayer and roll the lightest of three colors randomly over the stamped image. Remove some of the masks and repeat with the medium color.

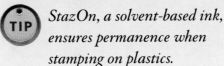
TIP *StazOn, a solvent-based ink, ensures permanence when stamping on plastics.*

4. Stamp the message on a smaller piece of transparency and glue to a painted frame, adhering on the masked area of the transparency. Attach the transparency to the card with eyelets.

5. Remove the remaining masks and brayer the darkest color, filling the entire transparency.

BEAUTIFUL MOMENTS IN TIME

WATCH CRYSTAL MEMORY PAGE | *Shelley Fuhr*

From Venice, With Love—St. Mark's Square, July 2004. A dial of twelve beautiful moments of a summer's day in Venice—feeding the pigeons, eating gelati, shopping for the perfect Venetian mask—all part of a family's magical vacation. Cropped and arranged around a clock face, the images are highlighted with acrylic half-moon watch crystals that draw the eye to the focal point. The old-fashioned numerals and clock hands, the clock-face palette of metallic gold, white, and black, and the black-and-gold frame provide a sophisticated base for the color images of a family enjoying an amazing day.

FREE TIME

ACRYLIC ACCENTS | *Marla Kress, Kim Smith*

The perfect send-off cards for a tropical vacation or summer at the beach. Tiny painted acrylic word charms, a vellum- sticker alphabet, a transparency frame layer, a ribbon-wrapped photo-slide-frame (on cards from Marla Kress), and tiny buttons on a summer shirt (from Kim Smith) adorn the cards.

MIRROR, MIRROR

SCRAPBOOK PAGES | *Shelley Fuhr*

With a full title of "Mirror, mirror on the wall, I am grateful for it all," this scrapbook artist celebrates all that life has to offer—inspired by and dedicated to a shop with beautiful roses in Cape Town, South Africa. The artist responded to the beauty and power of the roses, and that stimulated her interest in creating a page around them as a metaphor for her own life. She photographed the roses in the shop, and found the mirror mosaics in a shop nearby. The luscious backgrounds are painted with oil on paper. Ribbons, bows, frills, rickrack, beautiful soft colors and brilliant flowers, little oval metal frames and the 1-inch square mirror pieces create colorful, dimensional pages. The ribbon and rickrack borders and frames reiterate the colors of the roses themselves. (See page 80.)

ITALIA

ARTIST'S JOURNAL | *Alexis Seabrook*

We asked an artist who often works in watercolor to embellish some of her sketchbook or journal pages. She willingly obliged and created some stunning work with a great sense of experiment and fun. These beautiful old walls and arches of stone are studded with glass jewels, a piece of an old photograph of a serious child, and a heart-shaped charm in a marvelous gesture of intriguing playfulness. Miniature postcards with dimensional die-cut objects add additional contrast and color.

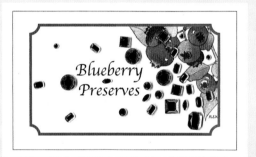

PRESERVE IT

HANDPAINTED AND EMBELLISHED JAR LABELS | *Alexis Seabrook*

Handmade labels for handmade jars of treats for good friends. The ingredients may be savored, but the beautifully labeled jars will become collector's items! This artist used parts of drawings she had done for another project, and added adhesive-jewel accents. Look at things with fresh eyes and an open mind. You never know where you will get your inspiration.

SHINING DROPS

JEWEL-ACCENTED GIFT TAGS | *Alexis Seabrook*

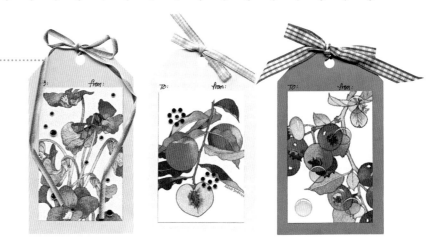

Sometimes the gift wrap or gift tag is as exciting as the gift. Or sometimes the gift wrap or tag *is* the gift. Gorgeous flowers, fresh peaches, and blueberries are the basic elements for these charming gift tags. Maybe the gift is fruit jelly or preserves, or fresh flowers or fruit. It does not matter. The tags have made a real statement.

ITALIA II

TRAVEL JOURNAL | *Alexis Seabrook*

An ornamented colonnaded portico is surrounded with glass-bead flowers, metal flowers and charm, a metal dove, old cancelled stamps, and an old postcard all in soft aged tones. The composition itself is a tall, ornamented column. A sense of adventure brings good things.

Metal

Metal accents are hard to resist. They provide fabulous contrast to scrapbook pages, cards, giftwrap, and other paper crafts. Soft paper with torn, undulating edges offers the perfect stage for the stark dramatic statement of metal, from mesh panels to alphabet charms to brads, eyelets, and wire clips, from eyelet tags to eyelet quotes, and on and on. The variety is amazing.

Incised metal tags can be painted to coordinate with the palette of your project. Apply the color, and then rub the paint off the tag surface and down into the incised letters for an interesting textural effect.

String beads on copper wires and wrap them around a frame for a classic dimensional accent. Brads of many sizes, colors, and shapes are available. Some of our favorites are tiny flowers that sit beautifully atop a hand-drawn stem. And metal stickers provide delicate finishing touches to our projects. A metal tag can hang from a scrapbook page or card as gracefully as a bracelet from a wrist.

Who would have thought that we would use tin-can lids or bottle caps in our memory projects? But look how appealing they are, a glimpse into a time past.

CHERISH

COLOR-ENHANCED METALLIC STICKER CARD |
Marie-France Perron

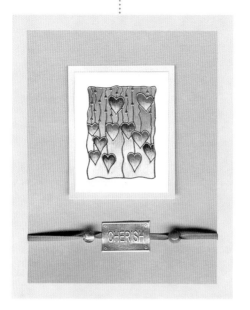

*S*oothing green hues are complemented by lavender and turquoise hearts amid a ripple of silver strings. The word "CHERISH" on a metal sticker centered on a beaded ribbon can be seen as a charm on a bracelet given by a best friend. Perfect for teens! Or it can be seen as a message framed quietly by a beaded ribbon. An appealing card from Magenta for young and old alike.

Creating the Project

1. Adhere metallic sticker on white cardstock panel and layer on a slightly larger soft-green mat. Color inside the sticker with colored pencil. Attach the matted panel to the card with foam adhesive.

2. Lace beads onto the ribbon and attach the ends behind the card. Add the metal word sticker at the center.

THREE FLOWERS

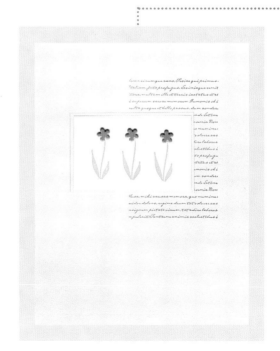

CARD | *Dave Brethauer*

A simple stamped motif can be amazingly elegant. The color and scale of this card are just right. The tiny flower brads add dimension to the rhythmic stems.

Creating the Project

1. Stamp the text in the upper-right section of the card.

2. Stamp three flower stems in green on white cardstock. Add the mini-flower-head brads.

3. Cut and layer the white cardstock on a pale-green mat, and mount on the card front inserted into the column of text.

SURFER GIRL

METAL-ACCENTED SCRAPBOOK PAGE | *Shelley Cartwright*

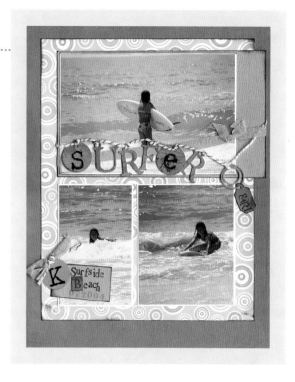

*P*hotographs of gorgeous turquoise ocean waves are echoed in the hues of metal letter embellishments. A wonderful way to celebrate a young girl's surfing experience!

Creating the Project

1. Ink edges of cardstock and patterned paper and glue to the center of the page.

2. Create embellishments on the large matted photo by painting metal letters and tying them to fibers. Stamp a mini tag, hang it on a metal clip, and add to the fiber "rope."

3. Stamp text on a green panel, and decorate with a blue "B" panel. Adhere to the lower-left photo with a metal alphabet tag and more fibers.

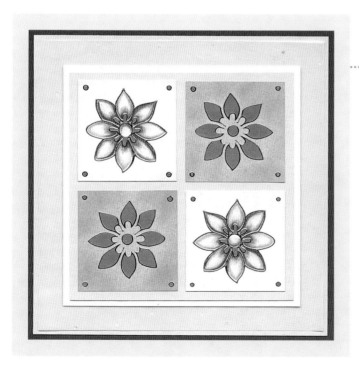

FOUR FLOWERS

POSITIVE-NEGATIVE STICKERS | *Nathalie Métivier*

A single floral design from Magenta is presented in two attractive colors, offset diagonally with mini brad stickers on a triple-matted frame. A lovely card for Mother's Day or birthday!

Creating the Project

1. Layer the front of the card with three various-sized cardstock mats.

2. Cut four squares to fit on the top mat.

3. Remove the positive shapes from two flower stickers and place them diagonally on the squares. Place the negative shapes diagonally in the other direction on the squares. Place mini brad stickers in the four corners of each square.

4. Accent the "negative" flower stickers with colored pencils.

LOVE

METALLIC HEARTS CARD | *Marie-Eve Trudeau*

*C*olored pencil accents the Magenta heart images shown here. A metallic sticker borders the featured rectangle shape. A metallic border of hearts supports the metallic word-sticker, "LOVE." A double layer of torn paper mats adds interesting texture. A genuinely lovely design!

Creating the Project

1. Stamp the three panels of hearts. Using colored pencils, color the images inside the centered panels. Add a metallic sticker border.

2. Tear around the design and attach the heart panel on a second torn cardstock mat. Attach to the card with foam adhesive.

3. Apply the metal sticker border below the featured image, and center a metallic word-sticker.

SNOW

STENCILS, LETTERS, AND WIRE | *Shelley Cartwright*

*H*appy moments spent in a spectacular winter wonderland is the focus of this collaged layout. Metal wire coils, cut-out snowflakes, and huge, stenciled letters spelling "SNOW" bring a smile as wide as those on the faces in the photos.

Creating the Project

1. Stamp cardstock background randomly with foam stamp and white paint; let it dry, mat two photos with lavender cardstock, wrap fibers around the large photo and place it and the smaller photo on the page.

2. Apply crackle medium to stencil letters, let dry until tacky to the touch. Apply white paint on top of the crackle, and let dry completely. Back three of the four stencil letters with the same lavender cardstock used for the mats, leave the fourth one blank, and adhere to the page.

3. Stamp snowflakes in lavender ink on blue cardstock. Tear out and mount to the page on punched lavender circles.

4. Create the wire embellishment by wrapping wire around a wooden dowel, removing and pulling the ends of the coils, and flattening. Straighten the end of the coiled wire to use as a photo holder. Add additional fiber ties, a metal clip, and a photo anchor.

LOVE, LIVE, LAUGH.

CARD | *Jackie Hull*

*C*olumns of printed papers in lovely muted colors with gently torn edges run the length of the card. Three of the same papers are cut and mounted on small rectangular tags, each one stamped with a word. A ribbon column running down the left side of the card like a barber pole supports the stamped tags that are attached by smaller ribbons inserted through eyelets.

LOVE IN AN INSTANT

TEXTURED PAPER AND STICKERS | *Michelle Tardie*

A small, white shopping bag is imaginatively decorated with "distressed" corrugated paper and stickers in an intriguing palette. One of the things we love about this gift packaging is that you don't have to destroy it to uncover the gift. This way you do get to have your cake and eat it, too!

Creating the Project

1. Cut a piece of striped paper to cover the bag front, ink the edges, and adhere.

2. Cut a 5 ¾-inch length of corrugated cardstock and adhere to the center of the bag.

3. Sand the corrugated cardstock and rub ink randomly over the surface. Repeat.

4. Trim border sticker to fit.

5. Attach photo anchors with brads between the letter stickers.

6. Use a metal ring and safety pin to attach the heart sticker to the bag. Tie the pin with a ribbon.

BABY OF MINE

TAG | *Rachael Giallongo*

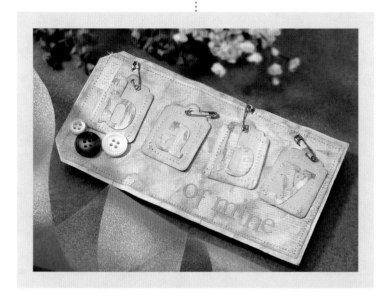

iny gold safety pins attached to tags are a delightful way to announce the arrival of a new baby! Soft-pink lettering on teal, on a background of whitewashed pink gives a feminine, old-fashioned, antiqued look. To antique the material, lightly crumple the tags and rub the tags and letters with distress ink.

Creating the Project

1. Mix acrylic paint with a slight amount of water and apply white-wash to all items.

2. Machine-stitch large tags together and the edges of the small tags. Apply letters to small tags.

3. Add pins, buttons, and stickers to the tag.

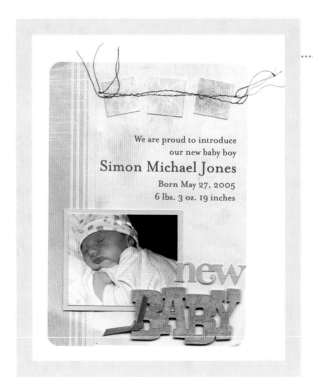

We are proud to introduce
our new baby boy
Simon Michael Jones
Born May 27, 2005
6 lbs. 3 oz. 19 inches

NEW BABY

CARD | *Marla Kress*

aby's first photo is black-and-white and accented with several blue high-lights. Blue stitching, a tiny blue ribbon, blue lettering, and a blue frame announce, "It's a boy." A birth announcement any new parents would be proud to send

Creating the Project

1. Print the announcement and crop into a 5 x 7-inch card. Round the corners of the card. Layer striped paper on the left side and machine-stitch floral paper squares across the top of the card.

2. Add the matted photo and sticker letters.

3. Use a paper towel to buff alcohol ink into the metal word, tie with a ribbon, and glue to the page.

SISTERLY LOVE

SCRAPBOOK PAGE | *Shelley Cartwright*

A loving tribute from the proud mother of two lovely daughters is displayed in a wonderfully sentimental design. The significant age difference between the two sisters is acknowledged by affirming how much each girl is unique, and loved and needed by her sibling. Metal embellishments include brads, a bottle cap, and stickers. Silk flowers, hand-painted lettering, and pertinent phrases encourage continued harmony.

Creating the Project

1. Cut a variety of patterned papers, inking all edges. Adhere to the top and bottom edges of the page.
2. Layer cardstock across the center of the page, tearing the lower corner of brown cardstock.
3. Attach various stickers, tags, and transparency across the page. Stitch buttons to the silk flower centers.
4. Embellish the page with metal words, frame, a letter, and a bottle cap.

CARD TRIO

3 CARDS | *Rachael Giallongo, Michelle Tardie*

F lounce and fun! Layered rows of playful papers, rickrack, and tiny metal tags remind us of summertime activities in a charming, cheerful card. The rickrack hides the seams of the rows of decorative papers. A well-washed denim jeans pocket carries a message of its own, along with the flower and metal tag. Generous amounts of pink paint were brushed onto the front of the metal tag and then wiped off when dry. The paint in the incised areas remains to highlight the words. (Both cards are by Rachael Giallongo.) Pastel color-coordinated eyelets add to the festivity of this delightful, bright-colored Easter card by Michelle Tardie.

FRIENDS

METAL-ADORNED BAG | *Heather Boling*

A special keepsake bag decorated with bright metal embellishments created with teens in mind! Every item in this design is metal, from the flowers and leaves to the lettering, clips, and tags. Creatively arranged so that it is feminine yet sturdy enough to last and be reused to reciprocate with a gift!

Creating the Project

1. Cut metal sheets with a die-cut system to create flowers. Spray entire flower with yellow spray paint, let dry. Cover flower centers and spray petals with red spray paint.

2. Run metal sheet through a crimper and cut leaf shapes. Spray with green spray paint. Attach with foam adhesive to wire mesh.

3. Attach alphabet eyelets.

4. Coil wire around a dowel and stretch, attaching ends to wire mesh.

5. Stamp text on metal-rimmed tags and attach with clips. Attach entire assemblage to the bag with brads.

HOLLY JOLLY

SCRAPBOOK PAGE | *Adrienne Kennedy*

A retro Christmas celebration is the idea of this design. Stamped in a dated font and bold black lettering on 1950s-style holiday wrapping paper, a black-and-white photograph of a Christmas from yesteryear brings back memories of family Christmases. A green Christmas bulb and brads for the lights are the metal embellishment here. A joyful, colorful way to remember the past.

Creating the Project

1. Center red patterned paper on cardstock background.

2. Stamp cardstock titles and tree. Decorate the tree with metal brad lights.

3. Adhere stamped pieces and photo to the page with foam adhesive.

4. Wrap the page with red-and-green decorative fiber and add a decorative brad.

BIRTHDAY GIRL

TRI-FOLD COIN HOLDER | *Michelle Graden*

*A*n ingenious three-fold album commemorates a little girl's first birthday party with photographs of party participants cut into circles to fit a coin folder. Metal embellishments include paper clips, a piece of cake with a candle, a bottle cap, a lid from a can, and a "Happy Birthday" sign—bits and pieces to delight any child.

Creating the Project

1. Cover the outside of a tri-fold coin folder with decorative paper. Peel off the top layer of paper inside the folder, and cover the surface randomly with acrylic paint.

2. Cover and back a stencil number 2 with printed-paper, staple on accent ribbons, and use a metal clip to attach to the page.

3. Fill random coin spaces with paper, photos, and painted small metal embellishments.

4. Place rub-on and stamped birthday phrases across the surface, adding acrylic text panels and a painted metal clip to a torn paper strip on the center page.

5. Use glue to mount a can lid framing a photo of the birthday girl.

EARTH TONES

TWO TAGS | *Becky Baack, Michelle Tardie*

*B*ecky Baack offers a unique way to say, "Happy Father's Day." And Michelle Tardie created an elegant rugged tag that looks like a ticket to a fabulous adventure! A hand-written poem, metal charms, and masculine earth tones set the mood for Dad to feel loved and honored on his special day! The postal stamp, elegant, aged handwriting in Italian, a mini map of Switzerland, and the twine give a feeling of packed luggage with trunks of wonderful memories!

THE PERFECT DAY

FOLDED ALBUM CARD | *Pam Klassen*

$\mathcal{A}$ card with wings, and a bright, colorful montage of "Mommy-and-me" sharing a perfect day together! The chorus line of metal keys helps symbolize the feeling that the key to happiness is simply being together. A delightful suspense ensues as the holder unfolds the purse-like envelope to reveal sumptuous textured paper, and the wonderful images of mother and daughter connecting joyously while a mother from an earlier generation is remembered. It is sure to be a treasured keepsake.

Creating the Project

1. Cut foldout pieces with the template on page 126.

2. Add papers, pictures, and die cuts to the inside of the pieces. Stamp the image and text.

3. Using a zig-zag stitch, machine-stitch the wings to the central square of the card through all thicknesses.

4. Attach the metal embellishments with brads to the card interior, and to the cover.

HAPPY CHRISTMAS

CARD | *Stacey Turachek*

Zig-zag stitching, a toppling tree, and a graceful star create a Christmas message full of light and warmth. The outline stitching on the tree (actually rub-on stitching) accents the slightly goofy look. Look at it and try not to smile!

Creating the Project

1. Stitch a wide, solid green panel across the middle of a patterned card.

2. Hand-cut a tree out of light gray-blue cardstock. Add rub-on stitches just inside the edge of the lopsided tree, and layer the tree over the panel and attach with foam mounting tape.

3. Add matching paper to the inside of the metal-rimmed tag and add sticker letters for the message.

4. Finish with adhesive gems and snowflake brads.

APPLES

QUILLED CARD | *Jan Williams*

Quilling is used here to create three attractive apples that sit on small metal stickers. Simple markers accentuate the leaves. This would be a pretty way to send a note to your child's teacher!

Creating the Project

1. Use a blow pen following the manufacturer's instructions to lightly color the front of the card. Or spatter paint with an old toothbrush. Add narrow strips of cardstock and a black line to the top and bottom of the card.

2. Mount three embossed metal stickers on slightly larger white squares and highlight the edges with a red marker. Attach the layered metal stickers to the card. Trace stems and leaves on the metal stickers with black and gold pens.

3. Create one quilled teardrop shape and six small coils for each apple. Glue on top of the metal squares and add a green stem and leaf.

TEATIME

SNAPPY GIFT WRAP | *Christine Timmons*

*I*ntriguing gift wrap from an artist who experiments to great effect with shapes, textures, and unexpected additions to her paper craft projects. And a grand sense of humor doesn't hurt. Fabulous purple matte wrapping paper supports a few light-blue, chartreuse, and black asymmetrical wrapping-paper panels; rubber-stamped images of undulating rectangles, steamy bubbles, and a fabulous teapot; metal snaps of varying sizes; and graceful arced lines drawn with a metallic silver pen. A wonderful carefree sense of motion with suggestions of The Mad Hatter's Tea Party. The message to paper crafters is clear: experiment and have fun.

ONE YEAR BOX

CHIPBOARD FILLED TIN | *Marla Kress*

A traveling, folding mini scrapbook with a single focus. What an extraordinary, imaginative way to create a memory box for someone special.

Creating the Project

1. Cover an Altoid tin with fabric and ribbon. Add stickers and a metal date.

2. Cut apart a dollar-sized coin holder to isolate six pieces with two circles each. Round the edges to fit in the tin. Paint the front and back of each piece.

3. Adhere the ends of two lengths of twill tape under the paper in the bottom of the tin. Space coin holders evenly down the length of the tape and attach the backs.

4. Fill circles with photos, paper, tag and ribbon.

ENGRAVED DRAGONFLY

LAYERED SCRAPBOOK COVER | *Nathalie Métivier*

A tinted dragonfly style stone is featured centerstage on this appealing textured, layered scrapbook cover. Wire, beads, a style stone, metal charm, metal clips, embroidery thread, maruyama paper, all contribute to a parade of embellishments. The sophisticated, glittery palette uses many layers and shades of green. It is almost impossible to resist touching every textured surface. Start building up layers of color by applying various shades of green and blue MicaMagic™ and fluid chalks to the surface. It is the layered colors that add depth to the palette. Mini Peel Offs add a delicate finishing touch.

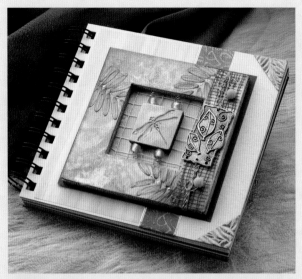

TIP *Use a skewer to hold the style stone while heat setting. Let cool in between steps.*

TIP *Use chalk, ink, or paint to color your raised image.*

SWEET, SWEET HEART

PIERCED METAL PANEL | *MaryAnn Klassen*

B eautiful pierced metal creates a delicate detail that glows as light shines through the evenly spaced holes. Embossing the hearts gives added dimension and texture to the design. Stamped die-lettering completes the message of love.

Creating the Project

1. Attach the template to metal with artist's tape. Place on a foam pad. Pierce through all holes, moving the template as needed to create the entire design.

2. Turn the metal over and position the template over the design. Trace the centers of the hearts with an embossing tool.

3. Turn the metal back to the front side. Position stamping-die letters and hit the top of the setter two or three times to set each letter.

4. Cover the card with patterned paper, cutting a hole in the center. Adhere metal behind the opening. Add brads.

1924

ROLLED TIN LID | *Pam Klassen*

A black-and-white photograph is exposed beneath an antiqued soup can lid giving it a dated and homey feeling. The year written simply underneath one of the rolled sections of the lid tells it all. A unique way to preserve a precious moment in time! (See page 104.)

Creating the Project

1. Punch a hole in the center of a tin lid and roll back the edges carefully, using a pliers.

2. Follow manufacturer's directions to antique the lid. Glue fabric, button, and flower to the front.

3. Stamp the date and back the opening with the photo. Glue tassels between the photo and paper backing. Slide a bead on top and tie.

CHARMED

CARDS | *Kortney Langley, Sherry Cartwright*

A fresh take on traditional sentiments. Kortney Langley trimmed a tree with metal photo anchors and a star-shaped button to top the festively garlanded Christmas tree with coiled metal wire. Sherry Cartwright hung metal charms off the bottom of a sales tag and transformed it into a funky message of love. A tiny photo of the person to whom the keyholder is dedicated hangs amid the charms. A happy heart is assured with this fresh, intriguing arrangement!

FAMILY

BOTTLE CAP HERITAGE | *Jenna Beegle*

*W*e are always thinking of ways to engage children in the sense of family, in their heritage. This splendid special tin is one way to do that. The tin is a great place to store little treasures, and a visual reminder of family members who preceded the current generation.

Creating the Project

1. Paint the tin with brown acrylic paint.

2. Rub areas of the tin with a thick coat of petroleum jelly and paint a coat of black over the entire tin.

3. Remove the petroleum jelly using a towel or rag. Paint that had covered these areas will also rub off, revealing the base coat. Rinse tin well to ensure all jelly is removed.

4. Punch eight faces from photos using a circle punch. Attach photos inside bottle caps using foam adhesive.

5. Stamp "Family" onto a bottle cap; cover with white embossing powder, and heat-emboss.

6. Center paper on the tin top and add bottle caps with strong double-sided adhesive. Use foam adhesive for the center cap.

 TIP *Use caution with needle-nosed pliers when heating metal embellishments. They can heat very quickly and cause burns.*

Resources

For products used contact your local craft or stationery store, or contact the companies for a listing of stores near you. Adapt materials for your own projects.

SUPPLIERS

AMERICAN ART CLAY COMPANY (AMACO)
(800) 374-1600
www.amaco.com

AMERICAN CRAFTS
www.americancrafts.com

AMERICAN TAG
www. americantag.net

AMERICAN TRADITIONAL DESIGNS
www.americantraditional.com

ANNA GRIFFIN, INC. (wholesale only)
www.annagriffin.com

ARTChix Studio
www.artchixstudio.com

ARTISTIC WIRE
www.artisticwire.com

AUTUMN LEAVES (wholesale only)
www.autumnleaves.com

AVERY DENNISON CORPORATION
www.avery.com

BASICGREY
www.basicgrey.com

BAZZILL BASICS PAPER
www.bazzillbasics.com

BOBBIN RIBBON
www.morexcorp.com

CAROLEE'S CREATIONS®
www.carolees.com

CHATTERBOX, INC.
www.chatterboxinc.com

CLOSE TO MY HEART®
www.closetomyheart.com

CLEARSNAP
www.clearsnap.com

CREATIVE IMAGINATIONS
www.cigift.com

C-THRU RULER COMPANY
www. cthruruler.com

Daisy D's Paper Company
www.daisydspaper.com

DECOART™, INC.
www.decoart.com

DELTA TECHNICAL COATINGS, INC.
www.deltacrafts.com

Design Originals
www.d-originals.com

EK SUCCESS
www.eksuccess.com

FISKARS
www.fiskars.com

Gin-X
www.imaginationproject.com

Go West Studios
www.goweststudios.com
HERO ARTS
www.hearts.com

JEWELCRAFT
www.jewelcraft.biz

JUDIKINS
www.judikins.com

JUNKITZ™
www.junkitz.com

K & COMPANY
www.kandcompany.com

KAREN FOSTER DESIGN™
www.karenfosterdesign.com

KRYLON
www.krylon.com

LAKE CITY CRAFT CO.
www.quilling.com

MAGENTA
www.magentastyle.com

MAKING MEMORIES
www.makingmemories.com

MARVYUCHIDA
www.marvyuchida.com

MEMORY BOX
www.memoryboxco.com

Michaels® Arts & Crafts
www.michaels.com

Mrs. Grossman's Paper Co.
www.mrsgrossmans.com
MY SENTIMENTS EXACTLY!
www.sentiments.com

OFFRAY
www.offray.com

PEBBLES, INC.
www.pebblesinc.com

PLAID ENTERPRISES, INC.
www.plaidonline.com

PRINTWORKS
www.printworkscollection.com

PROVO CRAFT®
www.provocraft.com

QUICKUTZ®
www.quickutz.com

QUILLED CREATIONS
www.quilledcreations.com

RANGER INDUSTRIES, INC.
www.rangerink.com

RIVER CITY RUBBER WORKS
www.rivercityrubberworks.com

RUSTY PICKLE
www.rustypickle.com

SEI
www.shopsei.com

SAKURA HOBBY CRAFT
www.sakuracraft.com

SAVVY STAMPS
www.savvystamps.com

SCENIC ROUTE PAPER CO.
www.senicroutepaper.com

SCRAPARTS
www.scraparts.com

SOPHISTICATED FINISHES
www.modernoptions.com

STAMPENDOUS
www.stampendous.com

STAMPIN' UP!®
www.stampinup.com

TSUKINEKO®, INC.
www.tsukineko.com

THE NATURAL WORLD PROJECT MATERIALS

PAGE 12
Slide Mount (Design Originals)
Texture Paint (Delta)
Sticker (Bisous, Pebbles Inc.)
Brads (ScrapArts)
Wire Mesh (Amaco)

PAGE 13 BOX
Leather Cord (ScrapArts)
Alphabet Stickers (Wordsworth)

Decoupage (Delta)

PAGE 14
Left: Stamps (Hero Arts, All Night Media)
Keys StampArt Jubilee)
Ink (Memories, PearlEx)
Right: Stamps (Hero Arts)

PAGE 15 TOP
Patterned Paper (Karen Foster)
Flip-Flops (Michaels)
Stickers (Sandylion)

PAGE 15 BOTTOM
Paint (Krylon)
Chair/Umbrella (Jolee's by You/EKSuccess)

PAGE 16 TOP
Wooden Flowers (Michaels)

PAGE 16 BOTTOM
Patterned Paper,
Die-Cut Quote (Daisy D's)
Wood tags (Go West Studios)
Ribbons (Bobbin Ribbon)
Brads, Pin (Making Memories)

PAGE 17 TOP
Paper (Ethan Kate Line/Scrapworks)
Stamps, 4 Chipboard, Mini brads (Making Memories)
Ink (Clearsnap, Hero Arts)
Wood tags (Go West Studios)
Liquid embossing (Plaid/All Night Media)
Ribbon (Offray, May Arts, Michael's)

PAGE 17 BOTTOM
Patterned Paper (Sweetwater)
Dried Flower (Natures Pressed)
Alphabet Stamps (Leave Memories)
Eyelets (Provocraft)
Mesh (Magic Mesh)

Ink (Clearsnap)
Nature Stickers (Pebbles Inc.)

PAGE 18 TOP
Patterned Paper (7 Gypsies)
File Folder (Autumn Leaves)
Ink (Ranger, Clearsnap)
Wood Frame (Go West Studios)
Chipboard Letter,
Brads (Making Memories)
Flowers (Prima)
Ribbon (Bobbin Ribbon)

PAGE 18 BOTTOM
Patterned Paper (Gin-X)
Wooden Frame (Go West Studios)
Number Sticker (Basic Grey)
Ribbon (May Arts)

PAGE 19 TOP
Patterned Paper (American Traditional Designs)
Wood Frame (Go West Studios)
Metal Charm (Making Memories)
Gold Pen (Krylon)
Ribbon (Offray)

PAGE 19 BOTTOM
Patterned Paper (Scenic Route)
Leather Frame (Making Memories)
Brads (Adorned Pages)
Alphabet Stamps (Leaves Memories)
Ink (StazOn, Clearsnap)

PAGE 20
Glue (Beacon Adhesives)

PAGE 21
Interference Paint (Golden Artists Colors)
Eyelets, Brad (ScrapArts)
Photo Anchor (K&Co.)
Ribbon (Artchix)

PAGE 22 TOP
Stamps (Hot Potato, Savvy)

PAGE 22 BOTTOM
Skeleton Leaf (Graphic Products Corp.)
Straw Paper (Be Unique)
Brads (ScrapArts)
Alphabet Stamps (Making Memories)

PAGE 23
Rub-on Letter(Making Memories)

Page 24
Fabric (Creative Imaginations)
Stamps (Ma Vinci's Reliquary, Making Memories)
Crackle Paint (Krylon)

PAPER
PROJECT MATERIALS

PAGE 28 TOP
Frame (Great American Stamp Store)
Textured Paint: DecoArt
Punch (Marvy Uchida)
Page 28 BOTTOM
Tag Album (7 Gypsies)
Patterned Paper (Design Originals)
Slide Mount (Design Originals)
Brad, Concho (Making Memories)
Ink (Ranger)

PAGE 30 TOP
Stamp (Savvy Stamps)
Inks (Clearsnap, Tsukineko)
Brad (American Tag)

PAGE 30 BOTTOM
Punch (Fiskars)
Label (Memory Box)

PAGE 31 TOP
Quilling Paper (Lake City Craft)
Speckle Brayer (Fiskars)

PAGE 31 BOTTOM
Chipboard, Alphabet Stencil, Acrylic Paint (Making Memories)
Flower Stickers (Stickopotomous)
Ribbon (Stamping Up)
Ink (Stazon, Tsukineko)

PAGE 32
Texture Paint, Texture Comb (Delta)
Paint (Making Memories, Deco Art)
Stamps (Stampendous)
Ink (Clearsnap)
Buttons (Junkitz)

PAGE 33 TOP
Acrylic Paint (Delta)
Stamp (Penny Black)

PAGE 33 BOTTOM
Stamps (River City Rubber Works)
Stencils (C-Thru)

PAGE 34 TOP
Paper (Close to My Heart)
PAGE 34 BOTTOM
Punches (Marvy, McGill)

PAGE 35 TOP/BOTTOM
Stamp, Stickers, Aluminum Embellishments (Magenta)
Threads (Gold Plaid Maruyama)
Inks(Clearsnap)
Gold Leafing Ppen (Krylon)

PAGE 36
Patterned Paper (K I Memories)
Acrylic Paint (DecoArt)
Clothespins, Flowers (Michaels)

PAGE 37
Stamps (Duncan Enterprises)

PAGE 38
Stamps (Stamp Francisco, Hero Arts, Anna Griffin/All Night Media, Penny Black, StampArt Jubilee)

PAGE 39 TOP
Patterned Paper (Chatterbox)
Stamps (Ma Vinci's Reliquary)
Ink (Ranger)
Negative Strip (Creative Imaginations)
Flowers (Making Memories)
Clip (Scrap Essentials)

PAGE 39 BOTTOM
Quilling Paper (Lake City Craft)

PAGE 40 TOP
Tag (DMD)
Stamps (Endless Creations, Hero Arts)
Variegated Quilling Paper (Quilled Creations)
Quilling paper (Lake City Craft)

PAGE 40 BOTTOM
Patterned Paper (Making Memories)

PAGE 41
Stamps, Stickers, Maruyama Paper (Magenta)

PAGE 42
Paint (Krylon)
Die Cuts (JoLees)

PAGE 43
Textured Paper (DecoArt)
Paint (Ranger)
Stamps (Making Memories)

PAGE 44 TOP
Patterned Paper (Gin-X)
Wood Tags (Go West Studios)
Brads (Chatterbox)
Rub-on Alphabet,

PAGE 44 BOTTOM
Quilling Paper (Lake City Craft)

PAGE 45 TOP
Quilling Paper (Lake City Craft)
PAGE 45 BOTTOM
Quilling Paper (Lake City Craft)

PAGE 46 TOP
Stamps (River City Rubber Works)

PAGE 46 BOTTOM
Stamp (JudiKins)
Stickers (Stampendous)

PAGE 47 TOP
Die-cut Hand, Chain (American Tag)
Stamps (Stampendous, Judikins)

PAGE 48
Oil Paint (Windsor Newton)

PAGE 49
Frames (HMF Frames)
Letters (EK Success)
Oil Paint (Windsor Newton)

PAGE 50
Quilling Papers (Lake City Craft)

PAGE 52
Punches (Marvy Uchida)

PAGE 53
Quilling Paper (Lake City Craft)

FABRIC
PROJECT MATERIALS

PAGE 56 TOP
Stamps (My Sentiments Exactly!)
Ribbon (May Arts)

PAGE 56 BOTTOM
Stamps (Hot Dog: Great American Stamp Store; Words: Printworks)

PAGE 57
Cardstock, Album (Bazzill)
Patterned Paper (Reminiscence, American Crafts)
Ribbon (May Arts, Offrey)

PAGE 58 TOP
Stamps (My Sentiments Exactly!)
Ribbon (May Arts)

PAGE 58 BOTTOM
Stamp (Heart: Hero Arts; Words: Printworks)
Punch (McGill)
Ink (Ancient Page)

PAGE 59
Stamps (My Sentiments Exactly!)
Ribbon (May Arts)

PAGE 60 TOP
Stamp (Memory Box)
Glitter Pen (Sakura)

PAGE 60 BOTTOM
Punches (Marvy Uchida)

PAGE 61 TOP
Patterned Paper (Daisy D's)
Magic Mesh (AvantCard)
Brad (Karen Foster)
Die Cut (My Minds Eye)
Fibers (Fiber Scraps)

PAGE 61 BOTTOM
Patterned Paper (C-Thru)
Transparency (Karen Foster)

Flower (Making Memories)
Brads (SEI)
Ribbon (Impress Rubber Stamps)
Metallic Rub-ons (Craft-T-Products)
Butterfly (K & Co.)

PAGE 62 TOP
Charm (Stanislaus Imports)
Ribbon (May Arts)

PAGE 62 BOTTOM
Stickers (Arctic Frog)
Ribbon (Adorned Pages)
Alphabet brads (JoAnn Essentials)

PAGE 63 TOP
Stamps (My Sentiments Exactly!)
Paper (Anna Griffin)
Ribbon (Creative Impressions)
Ink (Tsukineko)

PAGE 63 BOTTOM
Stamp (Hero Arts)
Twill Tape (Creative Impressions)
Punch (Marvy Uchida)
Ink (Tsukineko)

PAGE 64
Patterned Paper (Chatterbox Inc.)
Brads (American Traditional)
Sticker (Cloud 9 Design)

PAGE 65
Card (Keepsake Holder)
Punch (Marvy Uchida)
Ribbons (May Arts)

PAGE 66
Ptterned Paper (Ki Memories)
Tags (Pebbles, Inc.)
Stickers (American Crafts, All My Memories)
Rub-ons (Making Memories)
Ribbon (May Arts)

Complete)
Metal Letter (Scrapworks)
Phrase Stamp (Leave Memories)
Metal word (All My Memories)
Ink (Clearsnap, Ranger)
Acrylic Paint (Liquitex, Plaid)

PAGE 111 BOTTOM
Left:: Metal Tag (Go West Studios)
Patterned Paper (MOD, Autumn Leaves)
Paint, Heart Charm (Making Memories)
Top Right: : Eyelets (Eyelet Outlet, Making Memories)
Stickers (Embossible Designs, We R Memory Keepers)
Rub-ons (Junkitz)
Chalk (Craft 7 Products)
Ribbon (Impress Rubber Stamps)
Bottom Right:: Metal Tag (Go West Studios)
Patterned Paper (MOD, Autumn Leaves)
Paint, Heart Charm (Making Memories)

PAGE 112 TOP
Metal Sheet (Amaco)
Eyelet Letters (Making Memories)
Wire (Artistic Wire)
Rectangle Clips (Creative Imaginations)
Sizzix Die cut (Ellison)
Brads (Scrap Arts)
Transparent Spray Paint (Krylon)
Alphabet Stamps (Making Memories)
Ink (Amaco)

PAGE 112 BOTTOM
Patterned Paper (Anna Griffin)
Stamps (My Sentiments Exactly!)
Brads (Creative Impressions
Ink (Tsukineko)

Ribbon (May Arts)

PAGE 113 TOP
Patterned Paper, Metal Clips, Charms (Making Memories)

PAGE 113 BOTTOM
Left :Metal charms (Making Memories)
Ribbons (Embellish It)
Pens (Zig)
Right:: Tag (Avery)
Patterned Paper (Senic Route Paper Co.)
Decorative Brad (Making Memories)
Brads (C-Thru)
Vintage Stickers (Close to My Heart)
Walnut Ink (Fiber Scraps)
Foam Adhesive (Scotch 3M)

PAGE 114
Paper (Ex Imp Global, 7 Gypsies, Carolee's Creations)
Die Cuts (Anna Griffin)
Stamps (Making Memories, Stampendous)
Metal Embellishments, Brads (Artchix Studio, 7 Gypsies)
Ink (Amaco)
Paint (Ranger)

PAGE 115 TOP
Snowflake Brads, Jewel Accents, Star Charm (Making Memories)

PAGE 115 BOTTOM
Quilling Paper (Lake City Craft)
Metal Stickers (Magenta)
Small Leaf punch (Marvy Uchida)
Blow Pen (Stampin' Up)

PAGE 116 BOTTOM
Patterned Paper (Daisy D's)
"1" Sticker (American Crafts)
"Year" Sticker (DoodleBug)

Stamps, Metal Date, Brads, Leather Flower, Rub-ons (Making Memories)
Striped Ribbon (May Arts)

PAGE 117 TOP
Maruyama Paper (Magenta)
Dragonfly Style Stone: Clearsnap
Stamps, Charm, Pearlescent Paper Embellishment (Magenta)
Ink (Clearsnap)

PAGE 117 BOTTOM
Patterned Paper (SEI)
Sheet Metal (Amaco)
Piercing Template, Pad Piercing Tool (American Traditional)
Brads (Creative Imaginations)
Ink (Clearsnap)

PAGE 118 TOP
Rust Antiquing Solution (Sophisticated Finishes)
Tassel (Provo Craft)
Dried Flower (Pressed Petals)
Ink (Amaco)

PAGE 118 BOTTOM
Left: Cardstock (Paper Palette)
Eyelets (Scraparts)
Wire (Artistic Wire Ltd.)
Photo Anchors (Junkitz)
Right:: Patterned Paper (Mustard Moon)
Lace (Making Memories)
Bookplate, Brads, Ribbon, Eyelets (Adorned Pages.com)
Ink (Stampin' Up, Versamagic)

PAGE 119
Paint (Plaid/AllNightMedia)
Patterned Paper (7 Gypsies)
Alphabet Stamp (Making Memories)

Templates

1. Start with a square of paper, and fold in half. Crease and open flat. Fold in half vertically. Crease and open flat.

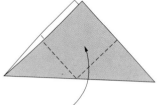

2. Turn paper over. Fold on diagonal line.

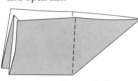
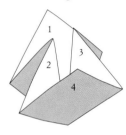

3. Rotate and squash the left triangle tip behind the front square. Squash the right triangle up behind the square.

SQUASH FOLD TEMPLATE, PAGE 15

THE PERFECT DAY TEMPLATE PAGE 114

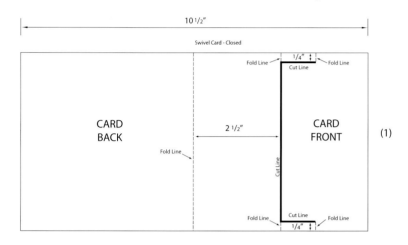

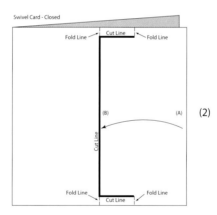

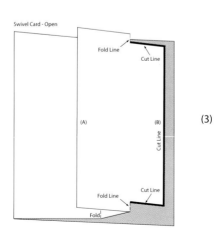

SWNEL CARD TEMPLATE, PAGE 41

Illustrated Glossary of Embellishments & Techniques

We are excited by the superb variety of embellishments and techniques available today. This glossary merely hints at the range of materials for your use. Adding dimension and texture to your paper crafts has never been easier.

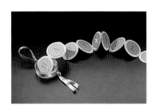

ACCORDION FOLDING
Accordion folding is a succession of alternating mountain and valley folds across a sheet of paper. You can make cards or small booklets with accordion folds. See page 34.

ACRYLIC FRAMES
Clear acrylic frames add dimension to your scrapbook pages and cards. Color and decorate them, or layer a frame over patterned paper for an interesting touch. See page 84.

ADHESIVE GEMS
Adhesive gems, available in many colors, shapes, and sizes, quickly dress up a scrapbook page or card. Use as a flower center, arrange several to create a flower, or accent a page in a random pattern. See page 103.

ALTERED BOOKS
Altered books are hardcover books that are turned into individual works of art by tearing, cutting, or folding the pages, and adding ink, stickers, stamps, punches, mementos, fabric—just about anything. See page 47.

BOTTLE CAP TREASURE ALBUM
Sized and cropped photographs fit inside small colored bottle caps (available at craft stores) offering intriguing shape, depth, and texture. See page 119.

CD CASE ALBUM
An artful use for extra CD cases is as a small scrapbook album. You can layer paint, paper, plastic, metal, wood, and fabric on the tin. See page 97.

COLLAGE
Collage is a collection of artfully arranged images, papers, or other materials, pasted together on a page or object. See pages 91 and 103.

BRADS
Decorative brads, eyelets, grommets, charms are small metal fasteners available in an array of colors. They are all used to great effect to provide interesting detail in paper craft projects. See page 90.

DIMENSIONAL GLAZE
Dimensional glaze is a water-based adhesive to apply directly over artwork for a raised lacquer-like finish. The glaze can be clear or colored; some variations contain glitter. See page 106 right. See page 88.

DIMENSIONAL PAINT
Dimensional paint is a water-based paint that can be applied to paper with a palette knife and combed through with different objects to create interesting texture. See page 32.

DIRECT-TO-PAPER INKING TECHNIQUE

Direct-to-paper is a technique of applying ink onto paper with an ink pad, Cat's Eyes®, dauber, or other inking tool. Pigment inks work best because they can be blended before they dry. See page 35.

EMBOSSING, DRY

Dry-embossing is the technique of raising or sinking an image on paper or thin metal using a brass or plastic stencil, and a stylus. See page 8.

GLASS BEADS

Micro glass beads will stick easily to double-sided tape, making it easy to add them to many paper craft projects. They add fabulous texture and sparkle to a project. See page 94.

HAND-PAINTED BACKGROUNDS

Hand-painted page backgrounds created with oil paint on the paper add depth and interest to the scrapbook pages. See pages 48, 49.

PAPER FOLDING

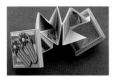
With just a few carefully placed folds, you can create imaginative three-dimensional objects of all levels of complexity. See page 15.

PAPER LAYERING

Paper layering can mean placing light paper, like vellum, over an image to screen or soften the image (see page 33); or adding extra detailing (see page 40); or framing an image by placing multiple papers behind (see page 38).

PIERCED METAL

Pierced metal (or paper) is punched through with a small needle A thin metal sheet can be pierced just as a sheet of paper. The piecing adds a delicate detail that glows as light shines through the evenly spaced holes. See page 117.

POPPING AN IMAGE

Popping an image is a technique of lifting the image off the surface of the page by placing foam mounting tape behind the image to be elevated. It adds dimension to the project. See page 37.

PUNCH ART

Punch art is the process of using punched shapes as is, or folding and combining them with other shapes to create new images. Both the positive (punched shape) and the negative shape can be useful. See page 52.

QUILLING

Quilling is an elegant decorative technique accomplished by rolling thin strips of paper around a slotted or needle tool into various shapes and then combining these shapes to embellish artwork. See page 50.

SHRINK PLASTIC

A wonderful way to maximize the use of your one-size stamp images is to stamp on a sheet of shrink plastic; cut and shrink it and you have a new size, a new dimension, a new texture. See page 92.

STICKERS

Stickers are quick and easy additions to a paper craft project. You can find alphabets and shapes in vellum, paper, fabric, and metallic sheets. See page 41.

TORN PAPER

Paper itself is an extraordinarily versatile embellishment. And the soft undulating edge of torn paper adds grace, color, and dimension. See page 17.

WEAVING, PAPER OR RIBBON

Weaving paper or ribbon involves interlacing strips of contrasting or complementary colors, textures, or patterns to create the illusion of woven fabric. See page 71.

128